The Garth Brooks Scrapbook

By Lee Randall

The Garth Brooks Scrapbook

By Lee Randall

A Citadel Press Book
Published by Carol Publishing Group

A Citadel Press Book
Published by Carol Publishing Group
Citadel Press is a registered trademark of
Carol Communications, Inc.

Editorial Offices
600 Madison Avenue
New York, NY 10022

Sales & Distribution Offices
120 Enterprise Avenue
Secaucus, NJ 07094

In Canada: Canadian Manda Group
P.O. Box 920, Station U
Toronto, Ontario M8Z 5P9

Text design by Leah Lococo
Photo layout by Karen Coughlin

Manufactured in the United States of America
10 9 8 7 6 5 4 3 2 1

Library of Congress Cataloging-in-Publication Data

The Garth Brooks scrapbook / by Lee Randall.
p. cm.
"A Citadel Press book."
ISBN 0-8065-1300-4
1. Brooks, Garth. 2. Singers—United States—Biography.
I. Title.
ML420.B7796R3 1992
782.42'1642'092—dc20
[B] 92-32036
CIP
MN

Acknowledgments

Without the endless generosity of the following people this scrapbook would not exist. My thanks to one and all.

Eddie Angel; Bob Braun; Steven Brower; the staff at the Day's Inn Convention Center in Nashville (especially Robert and JJ!); Mary Flanagan; Renee Walker Hall; Peyton Hoge; Lynne and Michael at Ink Projects; John Lamphier; Laurell's Mark and Zachary (great gimlets, guys); Mary Mancini; Michael Pietsch; Randy Piland; the staff at the Nashville Public Library; Ronnie Pugh at the Country Music Hall of Fame library; David and Janille Randall; Sarah T. Richmond; Debra Rosenman; Nona Jean and Jerry Sipes; Wiff Stenger; Joanne Van Cor; Jim E. Velvet; and (always) Josleen Wilson.

(photo: Peyton Hoge)

Contents

(photo: Peyton Hoge)

Chapter One
The Boy From Oklahoma

Early on April 22, 1889, a rifle blast sent more than fifty thousand people bolting out of Kansas into Oklahoma's Unassigned Lands to stake claims on 160-acre homesteads. At nine A.M. you'd have seen a train depot and a few shacks. By five P.M. it was Oklahoma City, population ten-thousand. In another month Oklahoma City was a thriving Midwestern metropolis, home to numerous lawyers specializing in real estate disputes.

A century later, to the twang of a steel guitar instead of gunfire, Garth Brooks made good on his Oklahoma roots when he burst on the country music scene with a debut album that catapulted him to stardom almost as speedily as the founding of his state capital.

Oklahoma, which means "red people" in Choctaw, is nicknamed the Sooner State after settlers who literally jumped the gun to cross the border "sooner" than its official opening. Though centrally located, Oklahoma's a relative latecomer to the Union, the last outpost of America's mainland frontier. In 1907 it became our forty-sixth state. Before 1889, Oklahoma was home to indigenous tribes and the "five civilized tribes" relocated there during the mid-1800s. Today its diverse population includes thirty-five Indian tribes plus a mix of Europeans, Asians, and African Americans.

Initially prized for its rich ranchlands, and subsequently its oil fields, Oklahoma's definitely a cowboy kind of place. Around the turn of the century Oklahoma was home to the world's most popular Wild West shows, basically cowboy-and-Indian circuses combining stunts and slapstick. Until 1985, it was home to the National Rodeo Finals.

One of Oklahoma's most famous native sons, Will Rogers, started out as a trick roper before hitting the vaudeville circuit and taking off as a humorist in the Ziegfield Follies. Oklahoma's also the home state of such performers as Reba McEntire, Roy Clark, Vince Gill, Conway Twitty, Patti Paige, and Woody Guthrie. Together with Texas and Tennessee, Oklahoma's considered one of the top three hot spots of country music appreciation.

So given Oklahoma's rich country music tradition and its legacy of speed, it's probably not surprising that America's *hottest* overnight success was born in Tulsa, on February 7, 1962. He's officially named Troyal Garth Brooks: Troyal after his dad and grandfather, Garth for his great-great-grandfather, a Civil War general. Garth is the baby of the family, number six behind siblings Jim, Jerome, Mike, Betsy, and Kelly.

When Garth was four the family relocated to Yukon, an unprepossessing town due west of Oklahoma City that grew up around the Union Oil Company. "I'm really proud to be from Yukon, and I mention it whenever I get a chance," Garth told the *Oklahoma Tribune* in 1989. Yukon, he says, "is an average city in the middle of average Oklahoma in the middle of average America." The family lived in an unpretentious split-level home at 408 Holly Street.

When Colleen Carroll and Troyal Brooks married, it was the second time for each. She had three kids and he had one; they expanded the family with Kelly and Garth. The Brookses are extremely tight-knit, so much so that a prefix such as step or half before a sibling name is tantamount to profanity. "We don't believe in that term. There were a lot of fights in town because of that term," says Garth.

Growing up, all the Brooks kids were conservative and well mannered and remain so to this day. Colleen and Troyal were a consistently strong, positive influence on their children—one Garth is openly grateful for. He remains close to his folks and speaks of them fondly and frequently during interviews. He credits them with providing an atmosphere that gave him the courage to experiment, to be himself. "My family is still my biggest influence," he boasts.

This isn't false sentiment staged for reporters. Marge Schuermann, whose daughter Tamie dated Garth for eighteen months during high school, says Garth's always been a devoted son. "He was really energetic and a good, clean-cut boy, even then. His main interest was that he was going to take care of his parents. Garth always said, 'If I make it big, I'm going to take care of my parents.'"

Garth's dad toiled for more than thirty years as a draftsman for Union Oil. "My dad was a Golden Gloves champ in the Marines in Korea, but he's the softest-hearted man you'll ever meet. If I could be like any man in the world, it would be him. He had six kids and paid for every one of them that wanted to go to college, although he never made over twenty thousand dollars a year until recently."

Colleen's a bubbly lady who clearly understands that presentation is nine-tenths of show business. She loves bright clothes and sequins. She wears her nails Dolly Parton long and frequently peppers them with paste-on sparklers or paints them with bold graphics. Back in the 1950s, Colleen was a professional singer under contract, ironically enough with Capitol, the label Garth would sign with thirty years later. Colleen was a regular on Red Foley's television show, "Ozark Jubilee," when Foley was one of country's top performers, though he ultimately died penniless in 1968.

Garth repeatedly says his mom gave up her singing career to raise a family. "She had six kids with me being the youngest. That's the kind of career she had. She gave it up when the last two—Kelly and I—came along." Sweet as her son's praise is, the martyrlike image started to rankle Colleen, who in 1991 quipped, "I said to him, 'If I read it again, I'll kill ya.'"

Earlier that year in *Country Music*, writer Bob Millard alleged that Garth's dad really put an end to her career after a family stint in Hollywood. When that effort failed to materialize in fame and fortune, Troyal shipped the clan back to Oklahoma permanently. Colleen contented herself by singing with her kids.

Garth is proud of his mom's musical achievements:

She's probably got the best voice of any woman I've ever heard. . . . I read some reviews Billboard *magazine had published. They were very good. They also had some video footage of when she was on the "Ozark Jubilee" show. . . . My mother lost everything she had in a fire. So for Christmas of 1988 I gave her copies of the news clippings from the files and a copy of the video footage. She cried when she got it. We usually get her Visions cookware or something like that for Christmas, but this was really different and special.*

Physically Garth resembles his mom, but his personality draws fairly evenly from both parents. As Colleen explained to Rob Tannenbaum in *Us* magazine, "He looks like the mother, but he acts an awful lot like *him.*" She pointed to her husband, whose reputation for being "bullheaded" has acquired mythic stature thanks to the media attention accorded his son. If Garth inherited sunny optimism from Colleen, he says his darker side comes from his dad:

If I could wrap my dad up in two words, it would be thundering tenderness. *He's a man with the shortest temper I ever saw, and at the same time he's got the biggest heart. Some of the greatest conflicts are not between two people but between one person and himself. He knows what's right and he doesn't have any tolerance for what isn't right, but at the same time he is so forgiving. . . . I learned from him that you gotta be thankful for what you got and treat people like you want to be treated. My dad drilled that into my head all my life. . . . We're a lot alike in that way.*

Another time Garth said, "My dad is one of the most loving men I've seen in my life, but

THE AGE OF AQUARIUS

Garth was born on February 7, 1962, in Tulsa, Oklahoma. He's an Aquarius—the sign of dreamers, the sign of genius, the sign of insanity.

This air sign is ruled by Uranus, and Aquarians orbit right "out there" with their distant ruler. Aquarians inhabit the future. They're ahead of the times, impatient for the rest of us to catch up. In *Sun Signs,* astrologist Linda Goodman explains that while most of us like rainbows, an Aquarian lives on one. "What's more, he's taken it apart and examined it, piece by piece, color by color, and he still believes in it." These guys are idealists extraordinaire.

You'll find Aquarians surrounded by a large, diverse coterie of friends. They're people people, though they tend to favor quantity over quality and have few true intimates. It's easy to get your feelings hurt by an Aquarius—they'll overwhelm you with attention, then wander off and lavish equal attentiveness on the next person and the next and the next. It's hard to keep an Aquarian's attention for long.

Though outgoing, Aquarians periodically hibernate. When they emerge, they're ready to play and make up for lost time. Aquarians hate being bored. In *Lifesigns,* Joyce Jillson writes, "It's true that when Aquarius is around, things seem to happen in big ways—of course, not everyone enjoys an avalanche."

Aquarians are gregarious iconoclasts who often "act out" just to stir things up. They like unusual folks, people with élan. They're analytical and incisive. Long after a conversation's over, they're still picking it apart, probing for hidden nuances. Aquarians ask a lot of questions—they're loaded with curiosity—and they always want to know *why.*

Aquarians are capable of steadfast loyalty to convictions they truly believe in, partly because they've thought them out so thoroughly. But don't expect an Aquarian to go to the mat for these beliefs. They're more likely to roll over and play dead, then when your attention's diverted, blithely toddle off along the same course they charted from the beginning. Aquarians are rarely violent, but they're not cowards.

Aquarians love honesty yet they have the gift of gab and are not above using it to confuse. Their honesty can manifest itself in a distinct lack of delicacy, and they're justly accused of being hypercritical. Sometimes Aquarians take themselves too seriously. Artistic Aquarians like to present themselves as eccentrics and may have lapses when they become strident or dish up platitudes as if they were news.

Aquarians are team workers who believe in fair play. They have high ideals, albeit of their own devising, and adhere to them strictly. Extroverted Aquarians have a burning need for visibility. They redefine the word *enthusiasm.*

Men born under the sign of the water bearer like their women a bit mysterious. Ignore him and he'll scamper after you to see what makes you tick. Goodman notes: "He admires a woman who holds her ground, if she's not too masculine about it, and if she lets him fly hither and yon, unencumbered by mushy promises and tearful accusations." An Aquarian male is not big on romantic gestures or naturally adapted to marriage. He likes his wife at home, doing "womanly" things.

Famous Aquarians include:

Abraham Lincoln
Franklin Roosevelt
Charles Dickens
Kim Novak
Clark Gable
Mia Farrow
Charles Lindbergh
Vanessa Redgrave
George Burns
Jack Benny
Galileo
Paul Newman

he's also one of the most feared because of the law he laid down. And my mom has always been happy just to see the next morning. She needs a lot of attention, and I think I got that from her." Garth recalls, "Out of all the things I remember as a kid, it was the attention I remember—to know that someone was interested in what I was doing."

Garth is an unabashed mama's boy and has been from the start. He told reporters that Colleen once showed up at school during track practice one rainy afternoon bearing a flask of steaming chicken soup, and hollering at him to dry off and change clothes. When classmates

ROLE MODEL

To no one's great surprise, all-American singer Garth Brooks is a huge fan of that all-American actor, the Duke. When Garth and Sandy spend a quiet night at home in Goodletsville, they're probably curled up in front of the VCR watching one of the many John Wayne films in their collection. Garth's feelings about the actor are so well known that members of Garth's fan club presented him with a John Wayne commemorative rifle and shells at the 1991 Fan Fair.

Garth's favorite Wayne film is *The Angel and the Badman*:

> ***My favorite part is the damn sheriff and the way he wears his hat. I guess I'm the only guy that wears his at an angle, and a lot of people stop me and say, "Your hat's on crooked," but the way the sheriff wore his in that was just unreal. His was eight thousand times more crooked than mine could have been.***
>
> ***I'd like to carry the same messages in song that [Wayne] did in his movies. He stood for honesty.***

taunted and called Garth a mama's boy, he retorted, "Yeah, and proud of it!" He often says, "If I have any talent, it comes from God and from her."

The Brookses raised Garth to draw strength from a higher power. He says, "I grew up in a family that never went to church, but they knew all the good things in life come from God. In no way could I even tie a good Christian's shoelaces, but I also know that all my gifts come from the Lord." Colleen explains, "I raised my family to love God, their family, and their country, in that order. Garth follows that to this day, and I'm very proud of the way he's turned out. He knows what's real, and it gives him an anchor."

She went on to say, "We're happy, optimistic people. We're kind of a strange family. We're loud." *"Very* loud," Troyal adds. This combination of carefree rowdiness and courteous good manners would set Garth's style for the future.

With six kids spanning a fifteen-year age difference, 408 Holly was plenty noisy. As Garth remembers it, the overwhelming presence was the sound of singing. "We had music around the house twenty-four hours a day." Though Garth wasn't much of a fan at first, his parents favored country music, especially artists such as Merle Haggard, George Jones, and Marty Robbins. By osmosis, if not by choice, Garth got a tremendous education in country fundamentals. His older sister Betsy loves Aretha Franklin, Ella Fitzgerald, Stevie Ray Vaughan, and Bonnie Raitt. One of his brothers adores Tom Rush and Dylan. Garth's influences were nothing if not diverse.

The Brookses had a tradition called Funny Night, when they'd perform songs and skits for each other's amusement. Garth's sister, Betsy Smittle, recalls, "When Garth was only two, he'd run into the middle of [Funny Night] and capture everyone's attention, and he's still doing that—capturing everyone's attention." Garth's first public performance came about in the fourth grade. He played a Fig Newtons cookie.

By all accounts Garth was a good, well-behaved student with a great sense of humor and an undisguised need for the spotlight. When the *National Enquirer* interviewed his fourth-grade teacher, LaDawna Urton, she said, "Garth was a classic teacher's pet—a teacher's delight. He did everything he was told to do, whether it was emptying the wastebasket or cleaning the blackboard."

Garth made good grades in high school and took an honors English course. His teacher, Patsy Woods, told an interviewer, "I remember Garth as a really good person, a big, warm-hearted kind of guy . . . he was a good student and had a good personality. A lot of students are shy at that age, but Garth was very personable, very comfortable with himself." During an otherwise ordinary reading of *Romeo and Juliet*, she said, Garth dramatized Romeo's death throes by sliding out of his chair onto the floor.

A jock, Garth hung out with his teammates from the football and baseball squads. He tends to downplay this bit of history, insisting, "I was the worst athlete that ever came out of Yukon." Mom brags that he was a football star, but Garth disagrees. "The reason I don't talk about it is because we were 0 and five. As soon as they replaced me [as quarterback], we had a chance at the state play-offs." When another interviewer asked about Garth's athletic prowess, he replied, "I tell you, man, I wore the uniform. That was it."

He once said his big failing as a football player was a distinct lack of aggression. "I never could get real forceful or real violent. . . . Even today, I never get upset. If I get mad or something, it usually scares me more than the person I'm getting mad at because I'm not that kind of guy. I've always been more of a 'head'-type player than I was a physical player."

Typically enthusiastic, Garth rejoiced in the school's success even when he was benched. Colleen told a reporter, "When his successor scored the winning touchdown in their sixth game, Garth was the first guy to rush out and help carry him off the field. . . . [He] was delighted the guy who succeeded him won the game."

Garth had long hair but he wasn't rebellious—just mischievous—and there was no sign of his trademark hat and boots in his teen years. Throughout high school Garth worked for the city park maintenance crew digging ditches and installing water meters. He made friends easily and mingled well, without regard for cliques or social status. Of course, to hear him tell it, "I was pretty much of a dick. Had to be the center of attention. Went from one girl to the other. I was pretty shallow."

He never took music lessons as a kid—in fact Garth didn't begin playing guitar until high school and even then he stuck to rock and roll. The first song he wrote was titled "Blue Rose." Naturally it was inspired by a woman. Was it any good? Garth says, "I understand where I was coming from, that's about all the good I can say about it." Still, it seems Garth has a tender spot for that title since he kept the name Blue Rose alive in his fan club and merchandising ventures.

His first guitar was a Gibson. "It had three strings on it, every other string. I added strings as I went along to keep from killing my fingertips. . . . A guy across the street wanted to learn how to play, so I promised I'd learn how with him. A couple of days after we started he quit. I didn't." Garth taught himself chords. He learned breath control and enunciation from Colleen.

When Garth was seventeen, he formed a group called The Nyle that played around town,

EARLY INFLUENCES

The 1970s were marked by a proliferation of mellow rockers whose work was characterized by an attention to lyrics that went far beyond "be bop a lula." Performers such as Jackson Browne, Crosby, Stills, Nash & Young, and the Eagles scaled the charts with songs that read equally well as poetry. Foremost among these lyricists in Garth Brooks's esteem are Dan Fogelberg and James Taylor, two of his all-time favorite writers.

I'm a big lyrics fan. The lyrics of the James Taylors and the Dan Fogelbergs just kill me.

Lyricists. That's it, man. You got three minutes to tell the world somethin', punch right through the chest, grab their heart, and say, "Listen."

Music is really for the heart and soul, yes, but it's also a teaching process, a healing process. I know whenever I'm depressed, I still go into a room and put on an album by Dan Fogelberg or James Taylor. Sometimes they make me downright depressed for a while. But that's what music is for, to create emotion.

I lived my life by [Dan Fogelberg] for a while and looked for answers to problems in his songs.

Probably one of my biggest dreams in music is to somehow work with or for someone to say I remind them of James Taylor or Dan Fogelberg. Working with those two guys is almost as big as my dream of singing with George Jones.

generally for free or for their dinner. At the time he was dating Tamie Schuermann, whose mother manages property in Yukon. Marge remembers letting the boys practice in the big upstairs bedroom of an empty duplex. "Garth always wanted to be a singer. The band was diligent, and he kept playing when he went to college," she reports.

The relationship with Tamie (who graduated a year ahead of Garth) ended after eighteen months. The *National Enquirer* quoted Garth as saying, "I told her all my dreams and tried to express to her how I felt. Then one day she turns around on me and says, 'Garth, I hate dreamers. I want a real man, one who's not living in a fantasy world of romance.' . . . Within a week she was dating a guy on the football team—and my heart was broken."

This isn't entirely accurate, according to Marge. She says the pair grew apart because they had very different post-high-school ambitions. Tamie—who never dated another football player, by the way—decided to go to nursing school, and today she's a successful RN.

Though classmates remember him as a sensitive kid who wrote poetry, it's doubtful that Garth was really walking around under a permanent black cloud. Marge remembers, "He was just a happy kid. Always a real gentleman."

In high school Garth favored rock and roll. He loved REO Speedwagon, Led Zeppelin, and Pink Floyd. He listened to Journey, Boston, and Kansas. Garth was also a devoted fan of James Taylor and Dan Fogelberg.

At a 1992 Garth press conference the subject of these early musical tastes came up. "Here's one for you, and don't throw anything at me," he said. "Through junior high I had every Kiss album there was. The late-seventies rock shows probably influenced my live show the most, the visual stuff."

After graduating from Yukon High School, Garth went north to Stillwater, Oklahoma, to attend the state university on an athletic scholarship, competing as a javelin thrower for the track team. "I majored in advertising through the school of journalism. I made a deal with my parents to go to college. I learned how to write jingles and be creative in what I did. . . . It was a big help."

People magazine said of the college-era Garth: "A cannon-armed 6'1", 225 lbs., he hurled javelins 200 feet and bench-pressed the combined body weights of Randy Travis and Dwight Yoakam—300-plus lbs." Another account has Garth an inch shorter, weighing in at 185—but whatever his dimensions, Garth's never been a weedy pip-squeak.

Garth and his older brother Kelly, another track competitor, roomed together at OSU. A college friend commented, "Those two were really close. They hung out together. It's pretty amazing to see two brothers be such good friends to each other." Garth echoed these sentiments when he told an interviewer, "I roomed with my brother Kelly, and that was special because we were already close, and it just made us that much closer."

Looking back on his college career, Garth says he has regrets. "I don't particularly care for the kid that I was. I didn't really care for myself at all in college. I took my parents for granted. I took my friends for granted. I've done some pretty stupid things—things I'm not at all proud of and that to this day I wouldn't want my mom and dad to know." Academically, he took the path of least resistance. "I did what I needed to get by, and if I could do one thing about college, I would listen to my dad more and study a lot harder."

Garth's appreciation for his father blossomed when he moved away from home to attend college. "I got out on my own in college and really saw what my dad has done. As soon as you step out on your own and start paying your own bills and stuff, you start lookin' to see how the old man did it with six kids. And you're probably makin' as much as he was then, you don't have any kids, and you're strugglin' to get by."

Garth also had his first close confrontation with death when his friend and coach Jim Kelly was killed in a plane crash. Garth took it hard. He was stunned and depressed and busted his hand punching a wall in despair. "I spent six months in a total blackout period. My whole life was black. I'd wake up in the middle of the night, out in nowhere, from just getting up and going walking. I remember just sitting on a swing set at three in the morning, crying my ass off and not knowing where I was." Ultimately, he dedicated his first album to Kelly's memory.

Garth held many jobs while going to school, and occasionally he worked as a bouncer. Nevertheless, he claims he's not much of a fighter. When a drunk challenged him to take their dispute outside, he said, "I was scared to death. I backed down. I felt pretty wimpy." He told another interviewer, "I used to be the biggest pacifist you ever saw. [But] sometimes the only things people understand are physical. I'll always try to do everything before getting to that point, but in the end, you have to fight for what's right."

Though he started picking at his guitar in high school, Garth admits, "I never expressed any interest in music until I was in college. Then I just got swallowed up in it." Now he began performing regularly. His first paying gig was at a pizzeria called Shotguns. Another frequent venue was Willy's, a sixty-seat club popular with Stillwater students.

In those days he had a full beard and long hair. He'd take the stage in whatever he happened to have on—more often than not a pair of sweatpants and a bill cap—and entertain the crowd with selections from a 350-plus song repertoire that included such tunes as Don McLean's "American Pie," Elton John's "Rocket Man," and Dave Loggins's "Please Come to Boston," a song he still plays. Garth earned $100 for those four-hour gigs and played six nights a week. Around this time he began working with another roommate, Ty England, now the guitarist in his touring band.

"College towns have a whole bunch of places where you can sing for money. I woke up and realized I was playing six nights a week. I couldn't think of anything else I'd rather do." Garth enjoyed singing so much, he nearly quit school when talent scouts for Opryland offered him a job performing at the amusement park. He discussed it with his folks, who struck a bargain with the boy. "[They] said they would support me, not economically but morally, in a music career if I finished college."

Garth's decision to be a musician got a big boost when he failed to make the finals of the Big Eight championships his senior year. "It should be the other way around. Your senior year you should be the best you've ever been. So I'm laying there on the high-jump mat, just disappointed as hell, and one of the lady trainers walks up and she said, 'Well, now you can get on with what you really want to do.' And that's when a big bell went off and I said, 'Hey, man, you're terrible at athletics, you're terrible at college. But the one thing you're proud to put your name to is your music.'"

Before this, Garth often shook his head in amazement at athletes who trained rigorously. "I couldn't understand why anybody would dedicate their life and time to one thing. . . . I didn't understand until I realized I was practicing my guitar four hours a day and playing six nights a week. And it hit me that this was what I'm dedicating my life and time to. Maybe this is what the good Lord has put me down here to do."

There was a little flack at home. "Mom tried to discourage our interest in music as a career. Her advice was, 'Don't get in it.'" Yet Colleen's thwarted ambitions had the opposite effect on both Garth and his sister, Betsy, now the bass player in his band. Garth sensed a certain mystique shrouding Colleen's departure from show business after releasing four singles between 1955 and 1957. In 1990 he said, "That was kind of like a secret, and a drive behind this whole thing. [I wanted to] really pick up where she left off and see if she can pass the stick on to me. Maybe she can live out what she didn't get to do through me. Because there ain't a day goes by I don't feel her right here with me. We talk on the phone just about every day."

Garth couldn't ignore the symptoms of a great passion. "I realized I got a lot more happiness playing six nights a week at a pizza parlor than I did playing sports. I'd spend all day trying to write a song, and loving it the whole time. So I figured, 'Why not take this more seriously?'"

Yet given his record collection and eclectic repertoire of songs, how did Garth decide to become a country artist, instead of a rocker? There was apparently an element of calculation in his choice:

I found that the James Taylors and the Dan Fogelbergs weren't respected as much as they used to be. People didn't take heed and listen to them as much. Taylor and Fogelberg were trailblazers, and they had a cult following, but I didn't want to work that hard. I wanted to go where lyrics could be heard and the words meant something, and that was country music. I've always loved country music because it allows the words to say something. I don't think there's any style better than country music as far as letting the lyrics stand out.

Garth claims that settling on country just meant adapting his style, not altering it. He correctly maintains that country's his birthright—even if it took him a while to cotton to that fact. Until 1981, to be exact, when George Strait had his first number one hit, "Unwound."

All those guys—like Journey and Boston and Styx—I had all of their eight-track tapes in high school, and that was my thing. But I couldn't sing that; there was no way. In the summer of my senior year I was driving to the store with my dad and this lady on the radio said, "Here's a new kid from Texas and I think you're going to dig his sound. His name is George Strait." And all of a sudden it hit me. It was like, "My God, I love this sound. That's it! That's what I'm gonna do!" . . . That's the exact moment it all changed. I became a George wannabe and imitator for the next seven years.

Visit Yukon, OK.

HOME OF
GARTH
BROOKS
and
THE
MILLERS
STATE CHAMPS
BASKETBALL "74 "79
BASEBALL "82
GIRLS SOFTBALL "86

Garth's celebrated on Yukon's water tower.

Now it's Garth Brooks Boulevard.

Garth's hat and shirt on display at the Country Music Hall of Fame.

Randy Adkisson

Garth Brooks

Michele Morton

Gerri Hill

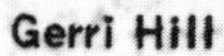

Gary Stevens

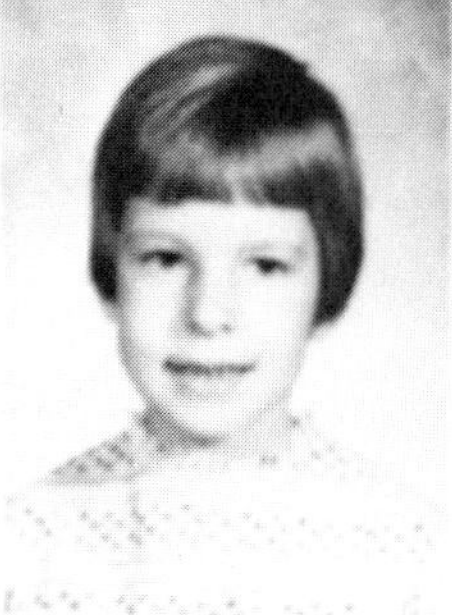

Val Fish

From Saturday matinees, two-wheelers and hopscotch to Saturday Night Fever, Trans-Ams and party hardy. Yukon High School juniors have really come a long way.

Greg Brehm

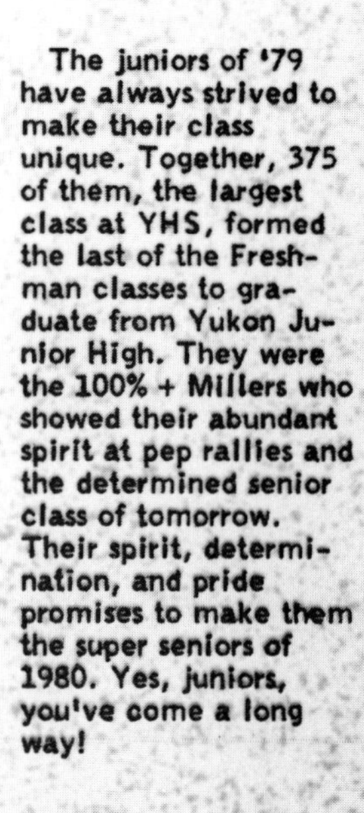

The juniors of '79 have always strived to make their class unique. Together, 375 of them, the largest class at YHS, formed the last of the Freshman classes to graduate from Yukon Junior High. They were the 100% + Millers who showed their abundant spirit at pep rallies and the determined senior class of tomorrow. Their spirit, determination, and pride promises to make them the super seniors of 1980. Yes, juniors, you've come a long way!

Terri Popp

Garth's elementary school in Yukon.

The house on Holly Street where Garth grew up.

Music Row headquarters of Buddy Lee Attractions, who book Garth's appearances.

The gates of Garth and Sandy's Goodlettesville Home.

Circa 1979, when Garth was a junior in high school.

The Original Class Of YHS . . . "JUNIORS!"

Mike Abernathy
Ernie Abraham
Arnold Adams

Mike Adams
Randy Adkinson
Billy Alexander

JUNIOR CLASS OFFICERS:
President, Cindy Prafka;
Vice-president, Robin Riddle;
Secretary, Lorri Cole;
Treasurer, Michelle Dugan.

Kelly Alexander
Jeff Anderson
Ailene Arnett
Teresa Atkinson
Tracey Ayers
Brian Banks
Lori Ball

Kerry Balentine
Laurie Banks
Libby Banks
Brett Bass
Kathy Beil
Lea Beilman
Jeff Belinski

Darren Benoit
Don Berner
Phil Beyer
Brent Biggers
David Beville
Sheral Bishop
Jana Blake

Michelle Bodine
Lori Bojarkski
David Bonner
Chris Bourke
Sandy Bowlware
Cheryl Boyce
Debbie Boyd

Anita Brauser
Mary Brehm
Greg Brehm
Debbie Bright
Belinda Broady
Bob Broderdorp
Angie Brodine

Garth Brooks
Karen Brooks
Ken Buffalo
Lisa Burke
Therese Burkhart
Rick Busby
Jim Buser

Miller Royalyt

Yearbook Queen And King

Miss Miller
Nancy Smith

Millerman
Brett Cory

Garth Brooks, Junior
Ginger Godwin, Senior

Candidates

Todd Thurman, Senior
Jerri Casto, Junior

Andi French, Junior
Gary Weaver, Junior

High's most popular students.

(photo: Retna)

Garth's all smiles at the *Billboard* awards ceremony.

Flannel-shirted Garth sits on the far left in the top row.

FCA: Athletes Joined In A Common Bond.

(top row) G. Brooks, K. Huckaba, S. Bowlare, M. Herbst, M. McCoy, M. Sills, T. Welch, R. Mathews, J. Siekel, G. Ward, M. Alexander; (row 2) T. Daniels, C. Simmonds, D. Harper, A. McRee, J. Ritz, L. Burke, B. Ward, D. Burner, J. Akin, B. Campo, (row 3) G. Constien, R. White, T. Soupene, P. Podolec, L. Wilson, C. Coffman, S. Greer, T. Thurman, L. Greenlee, M. Davenport, R. North, D. Taylor, (row 4) D. Merrit, T. Scheurmann, J. Banks, T. Merrill, K. Privott, V. Clovis, D. Bright, M. Mayfield, L. Cole, K. Gage, R. Jackson, L. Ball, D. Hoffman, V. Kinard, T. Lefler; (row 5) S. Willison, G. Manning, R. Daughtery, P. Compton, T. Ware, T. Burewell, S. Riech, D. Moyer, T. Burkhart, B. Jimboy, K. Lassiter; (Bottom row) OFFICERS: Dana Seelinger, Randy Davis, Boys' capt.; Nancy Smith, Girls' capt.; cott Layton, Robin Riddle.

The Fellowship of Christian Athletes is devoted to the ethics and ideals of Christianity among sports participants.

The organization, sponsored by basketball coach, Mr. Estes, invites inspirational speakers to address athletes. It also sponsors wholesome social events for students.

Each month a boy and girl athlete were honored with FCA Athlete of the Month. Pictured at the left are two chosen members, Brett Cory and DeAnn Merrit.

At the right Pam Podelec, Kevin Elledge, Larry Burgess, and Ronnie Mathews collect cans for the needy at Christmas time, this is one annual service project of FCA.

OKLA. STATE FAIR

Laugh through a thrilling ride. Scream through a chilling side show. Lose your money in a game of chance. Take an interesting visit to the arts and crafts buildings. When you're tired sit by a fluttering fountain and indulge yourself in fattening foods such as fried elephant ears and indian tacos. These are only a few ingrediants of the fun that the 72nd annual State Fair of Oklahoma offered.

Whether it was agriculture, hobbies, crafts, or just plain fun, fair time provided an opportunity for people across the state, including students from YHS, to gather and share their common interests. Below we see one of the many sights of the mid-way at night.

By Suzie Quigg

Val Patterson practices her skills on the adding machine in clerical office practice.

"A man's game" .... Garth Brooks and Terry McDaniel test each others strength as Robin Riddle and Shelly Elliot root them on.

THE FRIZZ!

What is it? A bird, a plane, no, it's, it's, ... the frizz! Hair fashions have changed throughout the years, from the 50's with ponytails and headbands, the 60's with bleach-blonde straight hair, and now to the 70's. Many different styles such as the feathered look, and the 'Farrah' have come about in the 70's, but now in 78-79, the frizz is the style!

There are many ways to frizz your hair such as pipe cleaners and perm curlers. Who knows, next year hair fashions may be long and straight, feathered, or maybe even the "LoBough" look!

By Ann Jacob and Kim Walkingstick

Wonder who won this test of strength?

Garth's second from right, top row.

Sports Spectaculars

Jane Clough won 1st place in girls' cross country for the state of Oklahoma.

Outstanding football players received their honors at the annual football banquet.

Enthusiasm for the atheletic program was shown throughout the year as shown by participation in pep rallies.

Above: Terry Burwell and Russell Spillers were the most improved runners for boys' cross country.
Right: Todd Thurman, Craig Blake, and Mark Davenport were named the all-tournement players for the Altus tournement.

Baseball was one of Garth's many high school activities.

(to the right) Senior members of the baseball team are; (standing) S. Johnson, T. Ware, R. Casto, T. Lefler, B. Brooke, (kneeling) D. Annler, K. Elledge, B. Riddle, K. Lassiter, B. Bailey.

Winter Weather Slows Team's Practices.

"We had a fine baseball team last year," according to Coach Larry LoBough.

They won the Mustang tourney, were runners up in both the Del City tourney and the Yukon tourney, were the Okie Conference Champions and finished off the season with a 29-19 record. All States' Special Mention went to Terry George, and Terry plus three other members, Jerry Wagner, Jerry Kennedy and Kerry Lassiter were Mustang's All Tournament players.

This year will be even better! Under the head coaching of Charles Teasley, the goal for '79 was to take State. He felt we were "an exciting team with a lot of speed and did score a lot of runs each game.

The rest of the coaching staff was made up of JV coach, Brent Clements, and Soph. coach, Randall Lokey.

The tptop players for this years team are K. Lassiter, S. Johnson, B. Brooke, B. Miland, M. Wood, T. Gaylon, T. Lefler, B. Riddle, B. Bailey, R. Casto, K. Elledge, R. Ross, J. Cooper, R. Scarberry, and G. Brooks.

It's a fly ball from "Beetle" Bob Bailey.

Junior baseballers; (standing) R. Scarberry, T. Galyon, G. Brooks, M. Wood, K. Wagner, J. Hill, D. Taylor, (kneeling) R Ross, S. Hyman, R. Morris, B. Cox, D. Stewart, J. Weaver.

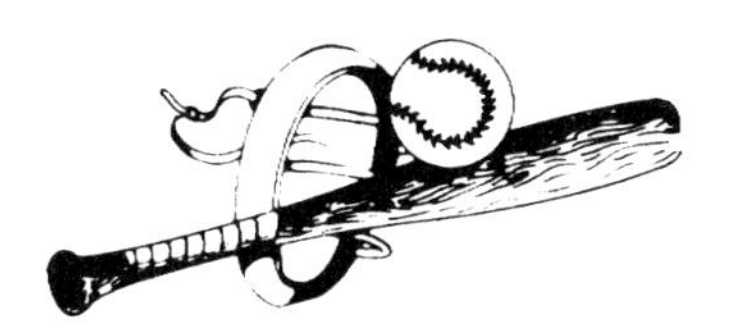

Watch that speedy arm of Kevin Elledge's in action. (In back is Bob Riddle).

Millers Go For Home Runs . . . .

Check out the second row from the top, seventh man from the right!

True Effort: Millers Kept Their Pride.

Top row: G. Ward, D. Mathena, S. Willison, F. Atkinson, R. Mathews, T. Welch, B. Ward, M. Herbst, B. Horne, J. Rogers, C. Johson, D. Williams, T. Daniel, S. Layton, G. Manning. row 2: Coach Lokey, Coach Kelsey, Coach Kusik, J. Russel, Coach Teasley, T. Jognson, M. Wood, J. Seikel, T. Lefler, D. Anneler, K. Hovde, G. McNutt, T. Ware, J. Ellerby, M. Dechant, P. Comton, M. Alexander, G. Brooks, B. McMurphy, Coach Clemens, Coach Lawrence, Coach Huckaba, Coach Campo, Head Coach LoBaugh. row 3: D. Holmes, Debbie Boyd, T. Merrill, S. Reeves, B. Riddle, K. Lassiter, B. Cory, R. Casto, B. Brooks, J. Belinski, B. Bailey, J. LoBaugh, R. Adkisson, K. Huckaba, T. Hildebrandt, C. Simonds, A. Forrest, T. Merill, A. French. Front row: C. Bornemann, K. Spencer, J. Buser, R. Buttry, S. Tillman, B. Howard, M. Campo, J. Cooper, M. Weber, G. Spillers, T. Elmenhurst, R. Daugherty.

After sixteen years of coaching at various schools, Mr. LoBaugh was named head coach of Yukon Millers football.

Coach Kusik ponders upon the next play.

Junior Class Of '79

Spirited juniors, Christy Lassiter, mascot, and Cindy Prafka, cheerleader, stare intently at an **exciting** YHS football game.

Decisions! Decisions! Flint Rector, along with the rest of the junior class, looked forward to getting their class rings.

Tony Torres
Lisa Tudor
Jan Tumbleson
Michelle Turner
Melinda Tyler
Kim VanAntwerp

David Vinson
April Waggoner
Ken Wagner
Steve Wagner
Pam Wallace
Jeff Stuart
Rita Stupak

Valda Sudduth
Kim Suitor
Bruce Suitor
Ricky Suitor
Shelly Webb
Mickey Weber
Tom Weeks

Chris West
Valerie Whitsitt
Bill White
Dana West
Tracy Wartchow
Gary Weaver
Jeff Weaver

Renee Webb
Doug Williams
Tina Williams
Matt Wood
Kathy Yanda
Jane Jenkins
Curtis Johnson

(photo: Peyton Hoge)

Chapter Two
Nashville for a Day

Though its chief industries are insurance, Bible publishing, and country music, it's only the last one that puts Nashville on the map for most of us. Dubbed "Music City USA" by deejay David Cobb in 1950, Nashville's synonymous with the Grand Ole Opry and the sound of country music.

Nashville was founded on the banks of the Cumberland River around Christmas, 1779, by a four-hundred-man entourage led by James Robertson, a woodsman from North Carolina. The Cumberland has excellent access to the Ohio, Mississippi, and Tennessee rivers, giving Nashville an exceptional advantage in those early days when boats and railroads provided most of the nation's transportation.

As John Lomax III points out in his book *Nashville, Music City USA*, from a musician's standpoint the city is almost perfectly situated. Based here, you're within three hundred miles—driving distance—of huge audiences in Memphis, St. Louis, Atlanta, Chattanooga, and other Southern cities. Extend that reach to 550 miles and you touch no fewer than twenty-two states!

Nashville's a quiet city filled with friendly, gracious people. Music Row, where the business of country music is conducted, spans an area roughly six blocks by four just slightly south and west of downtown. The main strip, Demonbruen Street, is lined with a tourist's mecca of gift shops and the Country Music Hall of Fame.

Off this thoroughfare are the peaceful, tree-lined avenues housing ASCAP and BMI, record labels, publishing companies, recording studios, music magazines, and other businesses catering to an entertainment clientele.

A couple of miles east of city center lies Opryland, consisting of TV stations, publishing companies, an amusement park, a theater, and a mammoth hotel—bigger than some small towns—sprawled across 406 acres. Owned since 1983 by Gaylord Broadcasting, Opryland is the current site of the Grand Ole Opry.

Why Nashville? It began on December 27, 1925, at the Ryman Auditorium. Here in the now-famous stately red-brick building the Grand Ole Opry made its debut on national radio. Every Saturday night since, it has brought a wealth of country music and comedic talent into people's homes. At first many Nashville residents—including a large proportion of high society types—were appalled by these "hillbilly" amusements, but the Opry caught on and has been entertaining us ever since.

The Opry offered country stars a weekly national showcase for their talents. Then, in 1942, superstar singer Roy Acuff founded Acuff-Rose music publishing here. By 1946 the city was bursting at the seams with singers, musicians, technicians, and suits. Capitol set up the first recording studio that same year, followed quickly by RCA, the first megalabel to open shop in the South. RCA got a big boost in 1949 by signing Hank Williams, the man most consider the greatest country musician of all time.

Members of the country music community are clannish and deeply suspicious of nonmembers. That's partly because they're still smarting from the sharp rise and equally swift decline of the *Urban Cowboy* craze in the 1980s. And country musicians are tired of being the nation's laughingstock, dismissed by "city slickers" as if all were hillbilly rednecks without intelligence or class. When Minnie Pearl steps on-

HERO WORSHIP

Garth is one of the biggest fans there is. He adores his heroes so much he'd be happier never meeting them, lest they be contaminated by contact with a mere mortal.

He's utterly devoted to George Jones, a country icon whose career and occasionally lurid private life have registered more than their share of peaks and valleys. Despite the ups and downs, scandals and triumphs, in March 1992 a *New York Times Magazine* profile dubbed Jones "by near unanimous acclamation, country music's greatest vocal musician, the equivalent to Frank Sinatra in saloon pop."

Garth's just one of many singers who adore Jones. Not surprisingly, Randy Travis claims he learned singing and strumming from the elder statesman's albums. But would you believe British rocker Elvis Costello is another ardent fan? Costello has written songs for Jones and covered "A Good Year for the Roses" on his 1981 country album, *Almost Blue*.

Jones, now sixty, was born and raised in east Texas. He dropped out of high school to sing professionally and has been performing ever since, releasing "And Along Came Jones" in 1992. Between his recording debut in the 1950s and resurrection as a living myth, Jones weathered stormy marriages—most infamously to Tammy Wynette—a cocaine/alcohol addiction, and a reputation seriously damaged by missing so many concerts people nicknamed him "No Show Jones." Now he's detoxed and out on the road, showing country's New Traditionalists how those traditions were forged.

How much does Garth love George?

No one, unless it's Jesus Christ with a guitar, is going to ever fill George Jones's shoes.

If I have a goal in music it's to mean to somebody as much as George Jones means to me.

The first time I met George Jones I cried. When I shook his hand, the tears kept popping out of my face. I felt real wimpy, but boy, I'll never forget that.

I know this embarrasses these two guys every time I say this, but I don't think an entertainer is anybody without his heroes. I love my Georges, George Strait and George Jones.

stage with a cheery "Howdy," people forget it's an act performed by a well-educated comedienne.

Like many industries, country music is incestuous, and nepotism runs rampant: talent alone doesn't insure success. As in most families, insiders gossip wildly amongst themselves but defend each other to the hilt if threatened by interlopers. This community doesn't welcome outsiders—and almost everyone is an outsider!

After graduating from OSU with an advertising degree, Garth lived in Stillwater for another year, working as a professional musician. He was the proverbial big fish in a little pond, a popular local entertainer with a steady income, a loyal following, and a terrific girlfriend. When he left for Nashville in 1985, he had plenty of friends to throw him a giant send-off bash and who chipped in to give him money and a monogrammed briefcase.

He didn't know the ocean's pretty frosty when you're swimming alone. With twenty-twenty hindsight he jokes, "There's nothing like an idiot with confidence. . . .This town shouldn't be named Nashville. It shoulda been named Reality."

Though he'd never been so far from home before, Garth was brimming with self-confidence, dripping with naïveté. "I pulled in expecting to see my name on every water tower around the place. . . . I was ready to deal it out, to really show these people how country music was done. . . . I thought the world was waiting for me. I thought all I had to do was open my guitar case and start singing and everything else would fall into place."

A friend of Garth's arranged an interview for him with bigwig Merlin Littlefield at ASCAP. Littlefield listened to his tapes but didn't get goose bumps. He dispensed some avuncular advice about the commitment Garth would have to make to succeed in Nashville. "He told me a person never gets rich just being a songwriter or an artist, and it was like a mirror dropped on the ground and shattered. I was sure that everybody in that building could hear my heart break. So I just stood up and told myself, 'I was a fool to come all the way out here, but I'll be damned if I'm fool enough to stay.'"

As if to illustrate Littlefield's point, their interview was interrupted by a famous songwriter—one Garth tactfully refuses to name—who came in to borrow $500 so he could repay a loan. Garth recalls, "That's when reality hit me between the eyes. I said, 'I make more than five hundred dollars a week playing the clubs at home. Merlin said, 'Go home. You ain't gonna make that here.' I walked out of there hating Merlin Littlefield's guts. Now I thank Merlin Littlefield every day for telling me like it was."

It's easy to be blinded by dreams. Maybe Garth didn't know that not so long before him another young singer named Randy Travis was rejected (more than once) by every label in town because they found him "too country." Travis's ultimate triumph might have given Garth's patience a boost. Instead, he nearly drowned in self-pity.

Like many a failed Hollywood starlet, Garth had come face-to-face with the realization that millions shared his dream—and frankly, partner, Nashville wasn't big enough for all of them. "I was shocked by the sadness in singing music. There's ninty percent sadness and ten percent happiness in this town."

Garth had a room at the Holiday Inn on West End Avenue not far off Music Row. He retreated there and stared out the window at a rainstorm that perfectly matched his mood. "I felt like every raindrop was laughing at me."

He felt overwhelmed by the prospect of establishing himself in a new town. Where to begin? "I sat there in the hotel room and started calling places to live, and the cost of everything was through the roof. . . . It scared me to death." Suddenly he felt very young, very foolish, and very forlorn.

THE OTHER GEORGE

Without the inspiration of Texan George Strait, Garth Brooks might not have settled on country music as his genre of choice. From the moment he heard Strait's first big hit, "Unwound," Garth's been a devoted fan. His reverence is so great, Garth's embarrassed to have outdistanced his hero in record sales and awards. When he shot past Strait to win the Academy of Country Music's Best Male Vocalist award in April 1991, Garth *apologized*: "I'm very happy but I'm a little embarrassed. I just want Mr. Strait to know he's always my male vocalist."

Garth praises George Strait frequently and lavishly:

> ***[Strait is] the undisputed king of country music nowadays.***
>
> ***I think the greatest compliment you can give an artist is to buy two or more of the same record because you've worn it out. It's happened to me on two records—and they're both George Strait records—Strait from the Heart and Strait Country. Those two albums tear me up.***
>
> ***Strait is a huge influence in my music, not in the music sense, but in hanging on to country music. During the Urban Cowboy thing, Strait was sitting there playing his country music when everybody else was coming out with these two-inch-deep songs.***
>
> ***I'm a huge fan of George Strait, and I can see how a woman could watch him stand there and sing for eight hours if he wanted to. Because he looks and sings great.***
>
> ***That guy rules around our house. When I heard "Unwound" that was when I decided what I wanted to do. I was a George Strait wannabe until Allen Reynolds pulled me over and said, "There's only one number one. Why try to be like him?"***
>
> ***I don't mind for people to call me a little [George] Strait—I'm a big fan of Strait.***

I was alone for the first time. At school I had my brother. When he graduated, I'd met Sandy, who took care of me. When I came to Nashville, it was just me. I just realized that I ain't shit alone. By myself, I'm just a loser.

When you are by yourself for the first time, you really have to prove yourself. You start looking down inside you, about what makes you up. You start pulling these things out to handle each adversity as it comes. I took a real good look as to who I was for the first time. I was made up of my family, the good Lord, and my friends. None of them were around me. There was something that kept me saying that this was what I'm supposed to do, but the time sure wasn't right. I was sitting looking at those motel walls. I made up my mind, "I'm going home."

He was learning that a tree cut off from its roots can't grow. "I had this trunk at the time. It was packed with all these things—like a metaphor for the parts of people that you carry with you. I realized that everything that I was, I left in Oklahoma."

Nothing truly horrible happened that day, but Garth expected to be "discovered" instantly, signed to a recording/management contract before nightfall. Like a lot of young adults—men in particular—Garth was phobic about the C-word:

Nashville screams for commitment. Everybody I talked to asked, "How long do you plan to stay in town?" I had this big fear about the word commitment. *[It] had been like a four-letter word to me my whole life. The idea of being committed to something or someone scared me to death. Since then, I've learned that a man can reach higher when he's tied down than he can when he's free. . . . That experience taught me one of the greatest lessons ever: you can't leave behind what makes you up, and that's what I thought I'd do. I left Oklahoma swearin' I wouldn't need anyone there again.*

After twenty-three hours, Garth bolted. "I'm thankful that I had the common sense to realize that I wasn't supposed to be in Nashville at that time." Garth hid at his folks' house in Yukon until he had the courage to head back to Stillwater. He wouldn't return to Nashville for two years. "There's nothing colder than reality. I wouldn't trade that experience for the world, it's what I needed, but I knew I was coming back."

The sexiest man alive?

Fielding reporters' questions before the show.

Thinking about the show ahead. . .

Rehearsing.

Wynnona and Naomi Judd congratulate Garth.
(photo: Retna)

Backstage at the 1992 Academy of American Country Music awards. (photo: Retna)

(photo: Peyton Hoge)

Chapter Three
Nashville Revisited

Garth was so mortified by his twenty-three hours in Nashville that he fled to Yukon rather than return directly to Stillwater where more questions would be asked. His mom was sympathetic and philosophical: "[Garth] got down there and they shut the door on him. It wasn't failure. He just didn't know the ins and outs. He had never really been away from home before, had never been alone."

His wits collected, Garth decided to head back to Stillwater where he resumed his relationship with Sandy as well as his minor-league musical career as a popular bar attraction. Sandy welcomed him with open arms and a strong dose of empathy. "He just wasn't ready. His heart was broken," she said of that first Nashville foray. He proposed to Sandy shortly after returning and they married on May 24, 1986.

In Stillwater, Garth hooked up with some musicians and formed a band called Santa Fe, which toured around Oklahoma, New Mexico, and Texas playing clubs and parties. "[We] played everywhere from the hard country clubs to the nostalgia clubs, where you had to know Dylan and Elton John and Dan Fogelberg songs. I think that was a tremendous asset—I think my music is a blend of all that and my country heroes like George Jones."

By the spring of 1987, Garth was ready to brave Nashville again. "If you're gonna play in the big league, you've gotta be where they're swingin' the bats," he explained, employing his favorite baseball metaphor. On another occasion he'd say, "As long as I've been dreaming about music, I've never seen failure in my dreams. . . . If you're not out there to be the very best, I don't know why ya suit up and grab the bat."

Clearly this was Garth's era for tackling commitment both personally and professionally. "I think my fear of commitment has always been a fear of failure," he admits. "Don't get me wrong: Nashville can be a cold city. It can tear your heart out and stomp on it. But this time I wasn't scared. I knew exactly what I wanted to do."

The difference this time was support, which came from Sandy and from the members of Santa Fe, who'd pledged to stick together for six months in a bid for stardom. Garth and Sandy roomed with the other members of Santa Fe temporarily, a design for living clearly doomed to failure: "You stick five guys, two wives, a kid, and a dog and a cat in one house, and try to see how you deal with the unknown. I'm telling you, it's scarier than hell. On top of that, we all had our own different ways of dealing with things. . . . It was fun for the first month, living with your dreams. But once again reality rang the doorbell. It just fell apart right in front of our eyes. . . . There were some hard feelings, but not as many as you might think."

Santa Fe disintegrated and band members went their separate ways. Garth earned money by singing jingles for such companies as John Deere and Lone Star Beer. He also sang demos and met country songstress Trisha Yearwood during this period.

Garth told *Performance* magazine what evolved: "I moved back to Nashville in June of 1987 and divine intervention was responsible for everything that happened that time. I stayed with Bob Childress, who was from Stillwater, Oklahoma, which is where I had come from, and the first night I was in town, Bob took me to a writer's night for a young man named Kevin Welch." Garth met songwriter Stephanie Brown

TRISHA YEARWOOD

She could sell oil to the Arabs with her voice.
—GARTH BROOKS

One of country's hottest female stars is Trisha Yearwood, whose very first single, "She's in Love with the Boy," went to #1, and whose debut album startled Nashville when it turned to gold.

Yearwood counts two influential Garths in her life—Garth Brooks and her producer, Garth Fundis. Trisha met Garth Brooks when they were among Music Row's most popular demo singers. Kent Blazy, who cowrote "If Tomorrow Never Comes," introduced them.

Trisha remembers Kent talking about Garth for over a year:

Kent said, "He's making an album right now and I think y'all would really hit it off." Kent booked us on a session together. Garth was still doing demos at the time. He didn't have a single out. . . . We did a couple of duets. We were singing on the same mike and doing the same licks and it was like, "This is really strange," and we really hit if off musically. It was like we'd sung together before, even though we'd never met.

Instantly, he was excited and said, "I think you're great. I don't know what's going to happen with my career, but if I'm lucky enough to have some success, I want to help any way I can."

A few years later, when the Georgia native landed her deal with MCA records, Brooks turned up to make good his promise. He sang harmonies on her hit "Like We Never Had a Broken Heart," which recounts the story of a one-night stand. What's more, Garth offered her the opening slot on his tour.

"That was a big risk for him and I'm so grateful for that opportunity because everybody wanted to be on that tour. I didn't even have a single out . . . and he'd never seen me perform live. . . . People make you a lot of promises and say they'll do things for you, but for somebody to really come through on their word and do it, somebody who didn't have to do it, that really said a lot about him."

Yearwood told reporters, "I've been really lucky to be out on the road with someone that I'd had a friendship with before—and who also happens to be the hottest thing in country music."

Initially Yearwood also worked with Garth's managers, but in 1991 she left Doyle/Lewis and eventually teamed with Ken Kragen. She explained, "I never actually signed with [Doyle/Lewis]. It was real hard to leave because they helped me a lot. And also my friendship with Garth, I was worried it would hurt that if I left."

Fame has its inevitable downside, the worst being the rumors that fly when you have such famous, influential friends. Trisha's faced a lot of brazen media speculation surrounding her divorce and gossip that she had an affair with Garth. More recently, people whispered that they're feuding. She takes these stories in stride. "I know that to people who didn't know the situation, it looked like I woke up with an incredibly bad case of PMS one day and wreaked havoc on America," she joked in April of 1992. "And if [people] read that Garth Brooks isn't speaking to me, well, I'm going to sing on his Christmas album tonight, as a matter of fact."

and went home to work on some tunes with her. Brown's name should be familiar as the coauthor of "Burning Bridges" from *Ropin' the Wind.*

Stephanie turned Garth on to Bob Doyle, who was an ASCAP executive until January 1988. Garth recalls meeting Bob on his third day in Nashville. "Bob told me he was leaving ASCAP and wanted to know if I wanted to go into business with him, so six months and a day after we met, November 16, 1987, Bob signed me as a writer to his new publishing company [Major Bob Music]. Two weeks later, he brought Pam Lewis in, and the two of them became my managers. We signed in January, and by April they had me a deal with Capitol."

That deal, formalized ten months after his return to Nashville, earned Garth a $10,000 advance—more money than he'd ever seen in one place in his entire short life. Even today that check stands out as an unforgettable milestone. In 1991 he said, "My last check was seven figures, but that didn't hit me one-tenth as hard."

This version of the events tends to telescope time, making Garth's already startling rise sound like the work of one fairly frenetic week. It *was* fast, but it wasn't instantaneous. Bob Doyle knocked on a lot of doors and heard a lot of nos before he had Garth well and truly launched.

More than once Garth's natural pessimism threatened to overwhelm him. He tells of the time he had to pull off the road because he was crying so hard he couldn't see where he was driving. "I thought we weren't going to make it. I thought we were going to crash, trash out, go into debt, poverty, all this stuff. It had nothing to do with the music; it was two people, newly married, struggling against debt. I thought it was over. . . . [I was] sitting in the parking lot of a damn fire station . . . beating my head as hard as I could [against the truck] because I had snapped, and Sandy screaming at me to quit. I was crying, she was crying. I calmed down, and we went back home."

Thanks to Sandy's levelheadedness—and her unwavering belief in his talent—Garth regained some perspective. She told him, "Now you're talkin' foolish. Set a time limit, five years, ten years. Settle down. Establish your roots. . . . I'm not makin' this trip every year. Either we're diggin' in, or we're goin' home for good."

When they got home from the teary scene at the fire station, Garth and Sandy found an advertisement for a manager's job at Cowtown, a boot store that stood near the Rivergate Mall just north of Nashville. Garth got the position and promptly hired Sandy as his employee. These were "the perfect jobs that fed and housed us for a year and a half." Once again Sandy proved an immeasurable help. She'd punch Garth's card on the time clock so he logged a standard eight hours, but he might actually be on Music Row auditioning or holed up in the back room composing songs instead of selling boots.

According to writer Michael McCall, Garth met his electric guitar player, James Garver, when Garver bought boots at Cowtown. That led to meetings with Steve McClure, who plays pedal-steel, and Mike Palmer, the percussionist for Stillwater, the touring group Garth formed and named after his college town.

In 1991 the *Nashville Banner* printed a funny story about Garth's days as store manager. It seems that Allen Williams, a senior account executive who sells radio advertising, handled the account for Cowtown Boots. A big part of the advertising business is wining and dining, so he took the manager and his wife to the Grand Ole Opry. Later, the wife told Mr. Williams she and her husband were leaving retail to devote themselves to music.

"I thought, 'Not another one,'" Williams told *Banner* writer Beth Stein. A few months later, when Williams phoned the new manager, she gushed, "Isn't it great about Garth winning all those awards?" Baffled, Williams had to be told that the pair he took to Opryland were none other than Garth and Sandy! Says Williams, "It turns out that the night I took them to the Opry, that was his first trip."

Eventually Garth's career did pick up speed. Bob Doyle tried generating interest in Garth at Capitol, but they passed. Luckily Garth had a second chance to knock their socks off. It was a classic "star is born" moment, when the scheduled entertainer fails to appear. Garth explains, "I was playing a showcase with nine other new faces in town. The producer of the show comes up to me and says, 'Look, the guy who's supposed to go on second isn't here. Would you mind going on in his place?' I said not at all, and Capitol Records was in the audience to see that act. That's how I got my deal."

The Bluebird Cafe is one of Nashville's prime spots for up-and-coming singers and writers to be heard by the music establishment. When there's a writers' showcase, the audience is full of talent scouts from the big labels as well as singers looking for new material. The showcase in question, sponsored by the Nashville Entertainment Association, occurred just two days after Capitol passed on Garth.

Nowadays most people associate Capitol's flamboyant president Jimmy Bowen with Garth Brooks, but the men who actually discovered Garth were Lynn Shults and Jim Fogelsong, in 1988 head of the artist and repertoire division and chief executive of Capitol respectively.

It was Shults who heard Garth at the showcase. Shults told an interviewer, "He did two songs. . . . He just nailed me to the wall, and everyone else in the room, too. I walked up to him and Bob right there . . . and told them that if you want it, you got a record deal right now as far as I'm concerned." Brooks remembers that night: "The people from Capitol came up to me afterwards and said, 'Hey, maybe we missed something.'" What they had missed was Garth's phenomenal stage presence, his ability to reach out to an audience, grab hold, and keep them enthralled, whether playing an emotional ballad or raising the roof with a good-ole-boy holler.

From the beginning, Garth was lucky to surround himself with good strategists and enthusiastic professionals who shared his vision. He amply credits his supporting team: "My whole thing was, who I surrounded myself with—managers and agents." Joe Harris, who books Garth for Buddy Lee Attractions, remembers his first meeting with Garth: "Jerry Kennedy had told me about this great new singer, so I told him to bring him up to the office. He did. And he brought his guitar. He sat there and sang awhile. I was knocked out, and I noticed people from all over the office seemed to gravitate to my door. You don't have to hit me too hard over the head for me to know something will work."

Harris lost no time drawing up a contract between himself and the singer. "Joe told us that no matter what record company we went with, he wanted to book me," said Garth in 1990. "We signed with Buddy Lee Attractions about the same time as the Capitol deal—with no product out. Then the first record came out after the [county] fairs had already been booked, so I didn't do any fairs. It's kind of amazing to go from that to doing one hundred fairs this year."

It's telling that Garth refers to his albums as "product," not art. His success is a primer for anyone studying merchandising, and many critics remind fans that his advertising course work shows. It's apparent when he talks about himself in the third person (most of the time), and apparent when you study the buildup that's made him a household name.

To keep Garth from spreading himself too thin, his managers recommended he curtail demo and jingle singing. They also minimized his club dates to create an aura of mystery and excitement.

As agent Joe Harris explained in *Performance*, Buddy Lee Attractions started pushing

THE REAL THING

Chris LeDoux is a country/western cult figure, a singer/songwriter who's also a rodeo champion and a bona fide cowboy. Since Garth mentioned LeDoux in his first single, "Much Too Young," he's been rediscovered. According to Garth, "His records are everywhere now. I got to play with him in Victorville, California. It's in the middle of the desert, a place called the Cocky Bull. We usually put on a real wild show, but we were fronting Chris and it's like, well, I'm going to be real cowboyish, serious. Then he came out and he's the loudest guy I ever heard. He just rocks it out, goin' crazy! I said okay, the next show we play together I'm pulling out all the stops. He's a great entertainer."

Chris's rugged individualism inspires Garth: "[Chris's philosophy is] this thing is going to go as far as it's gonna go, but he's not going to change what he believes in to make it go one inch farther. That's a philosophy now that I have taken on. I feel very good about Garth Brooks. If it means tomorrow he's got to do something he doesn't believe in or quit, he's going to quit. And I'm happy with that."

Though Garth's a big LeDoux fan *now*, he admits that the initial reference wasn't really his contribution!

"My cowriter, Randy Taylor, is a Chris LeDoux freak. Someone told me they thought it was just another cowboy song till I got to the Chris LeDoux line, and then they knew I knew what I was talking about. I didn't have the heart to tell them I didn't.

"Chris is a real cowboy. I love what a cowboy stands for. To me, a cowboy always stood for what's right. The same with John Wayne."

By the way, Garth loves cowboys, but wouldn't want to be one. Seems he's petrified of horses!

Garth long before the first album was recorded. "We started a year prior to finally going after dates by sending out postcards and mailers through Pam Lewis's publicity firm." Harris is adamant, however, that no amount of hype would ring the cash registers if Garth lacked the talent to back it up. "The bottom line has been the music. I was in York, Pennsylvania, with Willie Nelson before Garth's album was released, and I had a tape copy with me. I played it for George Moffett, who immediately wanted twenty dates. I knew right then we had a booking agent's dream."

Garth put these sentiments a little less delicately when he told a deejay, "You gotta be in the right place at the right time, but luck doesn't get you dick three or four albums down the line. That's going to take work, which I'm willing to invest. I'm in it for the long haul, which is the way it should be." Perhaps it's straining the parallel, but Garth *does* come from the state who's motto is "Labor conquers all things."

Prior to signing with Capitol, Garth made his demos with producer Jerry Kennedy. Kennedy wouldn't be part of his future:

I had been working with Jerry, and when he heard I'd been signed to Capitol, he told me he didn't get along very well with the folks over there, and it would be best for me to find another producer. I hated that because Jerry is a great guy, and I have a lot of respect for him, but I also respected his position. Capitol set up meetings with seven different producers, and Allen Reynolds was the first one on the list. After I met with Allen, I asked Capitol to cancel the other meetings if Allen decided he wanted to work with me. He took a week to really think about it and finally decided to go for it. It has worked really well.

Allen Reynolds is no neophyte. He's produced Kathy Mattea, Crystal Gale, and Don Williams among others. Garth says, "I believe every artist should have the pleasure of working with Allen Reynolds. Allen is in it for the music and believes the music will speak for itself. I believe he's right. My biggest compliment was Allen Reynolds showing confidence in me. He is one of those special few."

By Christmas of 1988, Garth and Allen were in the studio laying down tracks for his eponymous first album. Like all good producers, Reynolds proved an important influence on Garth's sound: "When I first went in to record, this Western opera voice came out of me. Allen sat me down and said, 'Just be yourself. If you hit, there's never been anyone like you. And everyone who tries to be after will be called imitators. If you don't hit and you're going down, at least you've been true to yourself.'"

Garth passes that wisdom along in his turn. "My advice is, 'Hey, man, it's your dream. Everyone's got opinions. . . . Listen to the people who want to see you succeed, plus listen to the people who want to see you fail, because you can learn a lot from them.'"

Choosing material is the most critical factor in Garth's estimation, and he was very selective about what went on this first disk. "I hate 'ear candy.' You can write it and make a living, but I want to get below the surface, to reach the heart of the listener. If you can't bring a tear, make someone smile, or change their life in some way, why write it?"

Garth's first single, "Much Too Young to Feel This Damn Old," was written back in Oklahoma between Nashville trips with his buddy Randy Taylor, who now works for OSU as an engineer and writes lyrics in his spare time.

Garth admits the rodeo tune was "the only song I brought to town with me that made it on the album. This tune best represents me—real cowboy music." He told an interviewer, "Taylor was a big Crystal Dew fan. He brought the idea to me and I started writing it on-stage during a show. There was just three people in there. . . . It's about being driven to do something that nobody understands what you're doing." "Much Too Young" got as high as #8 on the country charts. In 1990, ESPN used the song behind some of its sporting events.

His second single was "If Tomorrow Never Comes," a tender ballad Garth conceptualized one night when he watched Sandy sleep. Garth considers it the most honest song he's ever written. Before its release he said, "In my heart I believe it is a bona fide number one song. I wouldn't say this egotistically, but a number two record on this, or anything up from that, three, four, five, is a failure for me." Others were skeptical about the wisdom of releasing a ballad on the heels of his rollicking rodeo single, but Garth fought for the song and won. He had the last laugh when "Tomorrow" bounded into the #1 slot.

Garth says, "This song means a lot because of friends I have lost in the past. It makes the statement, 'If tomorrow never comes, have I done my job?' I passed that idea by a thousand songwriters until Kent Blazy realized the potential of the song and we wrote it." The song's about the love both men feel for their wives and also pays homage to Garth's friend Jim Kelly, and another Stillwater pal who died in a car accident in 1985.

Blazy says, "The idea he was trying to convey was something my mother had told me for a long time, about telling the people you love how you feel about them when they're alive. It really hit home to me because she had passed away about ten years earlier."

During Operation Desert Storm, Garth got many letters from American troops. "I'd get a whole bunch of letters with that big, round stamp on it. That's how I'd know it was from the men and women from Saudi. I thought for sure that 'The Dance' would have been their song, but it was 'If Tomorrow Never Comes.' It was the first big thing for them and their wives or husbands back across the water. That really makes you feel good."

Garth expected a big emotional response from "The Dance," one of his personal favorites, and the song he says signifies his entire career. "The Dance" was penned by Tony Arata, who wrote it to answer the question, "If you had the opportunity to change everything, what would you do?" Tony says he was inspired by "what if" movies such as *It's a Wonderful Life* and *Peggy Sue Got Married.*

Garth first heard the song when he shared a writers showcase with Tony Arata long before his first flush of fame. Tony recalls, "We did several writers nights at the Bluebird and Douglas Corner together, which is how he became familiar with 'The Dance,' hearing me do it. . . . Obviously, it made a lasting impact. We sort of lost contact for a while, and then, all of a sudden, we heard that Garth Brooks had been signed to Capitol, which was very exciting because we had known him before all that happened."

In 1989, Garth said, "For me, this sums up the whole LP, my life, and my music. It's a great tune by my friend Tony Arata." In 1991 he called it the greatest song of his career. "The Dance" went to #1 on the country charts in the summer of 1990, and Garth's innovative video for the song would win him awards throughout the year.

Tony told a reporter for the *Savannah,* (Ga.) *News*, "That [number one] status was by far the biggest thrill . . . you always worry that you're going to be the one to bury his career. It was an unbelievable experience." Naturally having a hit with country's hot young star was a career boost for the Savannah native, who moved to Nashville around the same time as Garth. "Perhaps people will be a little slower to pass on my next record," Tony joked.

The song that raised eyebrows from this debut album was "Every Time It Rains," which describes a brief interlude the singer has with a truckstop waitress. Garth fielded a lot of questions about this tune—everyone burned to know whether it's fiction or fact—and he answered without dissimulation:

I love my wife with all my heart, but the woman that song's about will know when she hears it exactly who wrote it. . . . [Sandy and I] have spent a lot of time apart even though we live in the same house because of that song. There's nobody else for me but my wife . . . but there was life before her that still affects me and my songwriting today. Sometimes it's nice to run back in the playground of my memories.

I tried to write it real generic to where it fit everyone's fantasy, but I tried to write it enough to where it could get you away from your everyday life and pull you into the story and stick you

FRIENDLY RIVALS—
GARTH VS. CLINT BLACK

It's almost spooky. Their birthdays are three days apart. Their initials are nearly identical. Their debut albums came out within minutes of each other. They've both been dubbed "New Traditionalists" and "hat acts." They both adore James Taylor.

Throughout 1989, Clint was the media's darling, and most put their money squarely on Black to win. After all, Black's incredibly handsome. His debut album was widely praised for its emotional depth and his terrific singing. Plus, Black was backed by the same high-power management team behind rock stars ZZ Top.

Those managers spent a million dollars to launch him, prompting the media to ask, "Will success spoil Clint Black?" Black's first album sold a million copies while Garth's languished around the five hundred thousand mark, and it seemed the kid from Texas had effortlessly outdistanced the kid from Oklahoma.

Yet Brooks's dynamic stage presence and equally strong marketing muscle prevailed. He released his second album, *No Fences*, while Black was still fine-tuning his. Black released another single, but Garth's second album was a blockbuster. And so was his third. To date, combined sales of the first three Brooks albums hover near the 20-million mark. Clint Black, while popular, respected, and successful, has never caught up. Of course, that's an unfair comparison—who could catch up to Garth?

Garth's often asked about Clint, and his replies prove how much he welcomes healthy competition. Garth has nothing but respect for the handsome, talented Texan chasing him up the charts.

1989 *When I'm compared with Clint Black, it's a compliment. . . . I think he's a very talented guy.*

1990 *I told him at the last awards shows we were at, I said, "When you came out, I hated your guts, probably simply because I was envious. . . . But I've grown to love you and what you stand for. I know it sounds corny, but if for some reason I'm not around, you take care of country music just the way you've been doing."*

It does bother me that some people seem to think that either Clint Black or I will survive, and both of us won't. Some clubs won't play Clint if I'm there, and I hate they see it that way. I hope Clint stays around forever, and I hope I'm here a good while, too.

I really tried to [hate Clint], but once you meet the guy you can't. He and his band are very, very gracious.

1991 *I have all the respect for him in the world. Unless I'm mistaken, he's a pretty sharp kid—and that's just what he is, too, man. He's just a kid. They're throwing all this in his face, and he's handling it the best that he can.*

[Clint is] a good-looking kid who has got all his hair.

If you want to know if the situation between the two of us is competitive, hell, yes. I smile when I say that. . . . People are sometimes confused when I say, "Thank God for Clint Black." Everything that I've worked for in the past two years seemed to hit him all in a month. I didn't handle my success very well as it was, although I have it together now. If everything hit me as quick as it hit Clint, I'm not sure I would have handled the ball.

in that roadside cafe while it was raining. But I didn't want to describe the people in it because you are the person—you are the woman and I am the man in it or you are the man in it and I am the woman—however you want to look at it.

It's hard to tell your wife that sometimes you have to write about things that happened maybe even before you met. On days like that, I stop off on the way home and buy frozen dinners 'cause I know that's all I'm going to eat.

Ever attuned to lyrics, Garth views music as a soapbox. "I'd like to have a musical feel that really feels good to sit in—and then while you've got 'em there strapped in, feed 'em some opinions." Whether the songs are gut wrenching or clever, he reasons, they can all impart a particle of wisdom and passion. "There's a million things you can say that need to be said,

RETURNING THE COMPLIMENT

In 1989 and 1990, Garth toured with fellow Oklahoman Reba McEntire, one of the top country artists in America. Not surprisingly, the two have a mutual admiration society going. Here's Garth on Reba:

She's just a very professional being and she makes me and my guys feel like kings. I can describe her in one word—class. When we did "Night of a Hundred Stars," honoring Katharine Hepburn, they showed clips of her, and in one she said something about the "bloom of a woman": "If a woman has it, it doesn't matter if she has anything else. And if she doesn't have it, it doesn't matter what else she has." . . . That, to me, defines Miss McEntire.

And Reba on Garth:

I really admire him. He has great instincts, and he is great at marketing.

There are a lot of artists who can sing but who can't impart the emotion and personality that make an entertainer shine. Garth pulls it off.

NB: On March 16, 1991, eight members of Reba's touring band and crew were killed in a tragic plane crash. Garth dedicated his September release,* Ropin' the Wind, *to "Reba's 'Crazy Eight,' to their families and friends. I wish God's strength and understanding upon you."

messages that are of common sense, of values, things people have to be reminded of."

Capitol's first press kit included two pages of Garth's "take" on each song. Here's what he said about the rest of the album:

"Not Counting You"   I wrote this for a woman, I didn't expect it to be on the LP. At first it sounded too swing, like George Strait. Now it's one of my favorite cuts. . . . We ended up giving a kind of rockabilly feel. Good opening tune, great for concerts.

"I've Got a Good Thing Going"   This song is special to me. I wrote it with Larry Bastian and my wife, Sandy. Of all the songs on the LP, Haggard could do this one, it's the most country. A very strong song and, I think, bigger than I am. I thought someone of stature could cut it, like Haggard. In this case the song is bigger than the artist.

"Cowboy Bill"   What can I say. Tear my heart out and throw it on the floor—that's what this song does to me. Larry Bastian sat on the couch and played it for me. I asked him to put it on hold for me and he never played it for anyone else.

"Nobody Gets Off in This Town"   This is not a down song and I hope it doesn't hurt anyone's feelings. It was meant to be a lighthearted song. It's one of the most cleverly written songs I've ever heard.

"I Know One"   Bob Powell from England came in to the studio one day, pats me on the back, and said, 'Big Jim Reeves tune.' I didn't realize although Allen swears he told me. I really started panicking then. We ended up giving it a Patsy Cline feel.

"Alabama Clay"   This song and "The Dance" are my two favorite songs on the LP. When it comes to this cut, crank it up to thirty-seven!

Amazingly enough, the debut albums from Garth Brooks, Clint Black, Lionel Cartwright, JC Crowley, and James House all came out during the same week in April! From day one, Garth was lumped into a group dubbed "hat acts" because of their ubiquitous Stetsons. Initially he was philosophical. After all, Garth understands people's need to "name" things they don't understand: "As much as I hate the label a hat puts on you, if you take it off, nobody knows who you are. It's damned if I do and damned if I don't. If I put it on, people call me George Strait or Clint Black. If I take it off, they don't know who I am. . . . [It's a matter of] how you relate to people. When one of my songs comes on, I want people to say, 'I don't know what it is, but it's sure playing with my heart."

Garth Brooks was fairly well received. *Music*

GARTH AND HIS FANS

The flip side of Garth's hero-worshiping streak is an equally phenomenal devotion to his fans. It's partly because he's walked a mile in their shoes—but more than empathy keeps him signing autographs long after most other performers have gone to bed. Garth's fired by admiration and gratitude for the people who've made him a superstar.

> ***When you sit there behind that mike and you look out, you're looking out at the people who actually let you do this for a living. The bottom line is, it's the people who let you do what you do, and so, for me, that's just a small way to say thanks because there's no way I can pay them back.***
>
> ***I want people to realize that Garth is here for them. He's here for the American worker, and he's here for the dreamers. 'Cause that's what he is: a guy who believes in workin' for a livin', takin' chances and followin' your heart. And that's the kind of people I want to play to. . . . My biggest fear in my life would be to let those people down.***

Indeed, Garth and Sandy have adopted a full-disclosure policy to keep fans informed. Whether you ask about the state of their union or his state of mind, you'll always get a direct, honest response. Garth says they're so candid with the press because he wants people to know who he is. "I talk about it to get the bull out in the open. This is us, this is what we do. We are not perfect, we are just like everyone else, trying to do better. I do it so my fans will know the truth."

More than the awards bursting out of his closet, Garth cherishes letters from fans that describe how his songs have touched them:

> ***You wouldn't believe the letters I've received. My awards on that song ["Tomorrow"] aren't the wooden ones or the gold ones, but the letters. . . . And the video. All the single parents across the nation. They come up to me after a show and say, "That's me and my boy's or girl's song" because that's the little girl or little boy in the video. Those are my rewards.***
>
> ***I'll try my best to keep up contact with the fans. You don't know how long you can keep it up, but you've got to do everything you can because the day you stop doing it is the day your career's***

Row magazine noted Garth's "strong, resonant voice and the requisite small-town, Southern background," but cautioned listeners not to hold those clichés against him. They found his performance on both swing tunes and ballads expertly achieved. And though this was a slick recording, they noticed his affability right away. "Brooks also has a personality that sets him apart [and]. . . songs that offer some new, courageous slants on traditional honky-tonk themes." Garth may have ridden into town on Randy Travis's coattails, they concluded, but he "thinks for himself, and he takes chances. He also just made the best of an opportunity."

Stereo Review approved of Garth's unusual collection of tunes, calling them offbeat and unexpected. "As a vocalist Brooks . . . has an easygoing, lasso-throwing pace that tends to compensate for his lack of a distinctive style, his big-boy timbre, and Reynolds's fairly stock arrangements." This reviewer also found Garth "immensely likable."

David Zimmerman, reviewing the album for *USA Today*, called it "core country with heartfelt, hurtin' vocals and country timelessness." The syndicated *Tennessean* writer, Robert K. Oermann, enjoyed Garth's first single. He wrote, "By-God country to the core. A hurtin' vocal, chiming steel, sawing fiddle and toe-tapping hillbilly beat. . . . I can tell you right now, just six records into the stack, that Garth Brooks has my heart as Discovery of the Day."

From the outset, some of Garth's biggest fans were disc jockeys, and he's the first to credit radio with boosting his career. In July he told the *Tulsa* (Okla.) *Tribune* that deejay Billy Parker of KVOO played his first single "the day he got it. Tulsa was a strong foundation for me because all the country stations helped. My family and friends called all the country stations. It really got the ball rolling for me."

A year later, in 1990, he told the *Ogden*

(Iowa) *Reporter*, "It's all divine intervention. . . . I would honestly have to say it was radio. Radio picked me up and took me in like a son. I don't know why they did and I don't even want to ask why. I'm just very happy they did."

It's said that country music disc jockeys respond as much to a performer's personality as to his music. Certainly deejays were responsible for keeping his first single on the air even when sales were slow. Since the business is self-perpetuating, the more a station played his single the more other stations played it, which boosted sales to consumers. "Radio has taken care of me like its own," says Garth thankfully.

Capitol included a full page of deejay raves in Garth's press kit. Tom Phillips of WDOD in Chattanooga said, "Just when George Jones asked 'Who's Gonna Fill Their Shoes,' along comes Garth Brooks." Jim Gibb of KTPK in Topeka, Kansas, called Garth "one of the best new artists in country music." Jim Mickelson of KKAT, Salt Lake City, Utah, said, "No pressure, no hype, back to the grass-roots sound. Country music needs artists like Garth Brooks, who delivers the lyrics with honesty and integrity."

One of Garth's big goals was to hear his own song playing on the car radio. The day it happened he nearly caused a traffic jam. Nothing beat that thrill. "It's just an amazing feeling that can't be equaled. There's two radio stations in Nashville. I was driving down the road and one of them was playing it. Then I switched stations and it was on there, too. I wanted to jump out of the truck and yell at everybody, 'Hey, that's me on the radio!'"

On June 24, 1989, Garth made his debut at the Grand Ole Opry, playing two shows at seven-thirty and ten-thirty P.M. that were broadcast live over WSM-AM. Just before the concert, at seven, he appeared on TNN's pre-Opry telecast. Ever emotional, Garth wept openly, full of joy to be on the show. A few days later Garth performed at the Writers Benefit Showcase for the Prevention of Child Abuse at the Douglas Corner Cafe.

From the start, Garth's concerts were energized affairs. "We play with very high intensity. We have the steels and fiddle, but there's an edge on the steels and fiddle. . . . On the album, the guitars are very clean. On-stage, they're a little fuzzier, and we've quadrupled the harmonies."

Throughout 1989 he toured the country, playing mostly opening slots for a variety of acts, including Alabama, Reba McEntire, George Strait, and Kenny Rogers. Garth whizzed about so much that first year, he barely knew where the bus set him down. "I usually know what city I'm in," he remarked, "but the other day I had to ask somebody what month it was."

Late in the year Garth had a cameo playing himself in a made-for-cable movie called *Nashville Beat* that reunited the stars of "Adam 12." Garth eventually watched the film and recommends the rest of us give it a miss: "It was a baaaad movie."

For all its difficulties, the first real problem Garth encountered on the road was a conflict with members of his band and road crew over the huge amounts of time Garth spent with fans. "The stage crew and band, they want to get out after a show. . . . But it's my fans who've put me here, and I don't want to forget that." Garth's so devoted he'll sign autographs until the last fan has left the stadium—even if that means sticking around until dawn. In essence, then, he performs on-stage for ninety or more minutes, then off-stage for hours longer.

In April, when someone asked Garth to rationalize his "overnight" success, he replied, "I wish I could say something magnanimous—but partner, I have no *idea*. All I know is that I'm sitting where I'm sitting right now, with my future in my hands, and that's just the way I like it. I'm in the big leagues. I'm taking my swings. And it's as fun as can be."

That first album produced four hits. "Much Too Young" peaked at #8. "If Tomorrow Never Comes," "Not Counting You," and "The Dance" hit #1.

All in all, Nashville the second time around was a helluva lot more fun for Garth, who never fails to deflect credit away from himself: "[I'm] so thankful to God and Sandy. It turned out real well for me."

Tearing up the concert stage. (photo: Ron Galella)

As the flowers testify, fans love Garth, and Garth loves his fans. (photo: Ron Galella)

Backstage at Bob Hope's 1991 special.
(photo: Ron Galella)

Strictly for the cameras, Garth escorts actress Sela Ward into the Academy of Country Music awards. (photo: Retna)

Garth sings on Trisha Yearwood's hit single, "Like We Never Had a Broken Heart." (photo: Retna)

With fellow heartthrob (and hat act) Alan Jackson.
(photo: Retna)

With the Judds at 1990's Country Christmas show.
(photo: Ron Galella)

Garth and his idol George Strait. (photo: Retna)

Garth's a fan of cordless headsets that give him the run of the stage. (photo: Peyton Hoge)

Chapter Four
Sandy

Behind every great man is a woman, the saying goes. Garth's doubly lucky—he's got two women backing him up. One is his mom, the other is Sandy, the lady he married on May 24, 1986. About his wife, he says, "When you look at Garth now, you see Sandy."

Sandy was born in Owasso, Oklahoma, in 1965, to John and Pat Mahl. Growing up she was a popular cheerleader and lifeguard. She graduated from Owasso High School in 1983 and briefly competed in rodeo as a barrel racer, a background she shares with Reba McEntire. At Stillwater she studied child-abuse psychology, but never got her degree because she married Garth and moved to Nashville instead.

When they make the miniseries of Garth's life, one of the most entertaining sequences will be his historic meeting with Sandy in the ladies' room of Tumbleweeds, the popular Stillwater club where he worked as a bouncer. He's told reporters, "I wasn't bouncing 'cause I was tough: I just needed the money." Unbelievably, he was the smallest bouncer on staff, so he handled disputes between female patrons.

"My poor wife has paid for this a thousand times," he says of their encounter. "A lot of people don't think she's very much of a lady, simply because of this story. But when I met her . . . she'd had a little too much to drink, mixed in with a little bit of anger." Another version of the tale has her "toasted on tequila."

Anyway, Garth tells it best: "These two gals had cornered her in the women's bathroom. She took a swing at this one ole gal and missed her. But her fist went through the pressed-wood stall and she couldn't get it back out. She was just madder than a hornet." It seems the girl who cornered Sandy thought she'd been messing with her boyfriend. Sandy reckoned she'd scare her and threw the punch.

"All [Sandy] said was, 'I missed.' I thought, 'Man, this is nuts.' Then I told her she had to leave, but as I was takin' her outside, I kept thinkin' about how good-lookin' she was."

Garth escorted Sandy from the club and told her a whopper—that it was part of his job as bouncer to see her safely home to the dormitory. Then he said his roommate was away and if Sandy wanted to stay at his place he'd drive her home in the morning. He laughs. "She said, 'Drop dead, asshole!' and called me a few other names and walked off. I thought, 'This girl's got class.' I said, 'Well, can I call ya?'"

Sandy jokes, "I turned him down. I think that's what caught his eye." They started dating and were still going strong when Garth lit out for Nashville in 1985.

In his book on Brooks, author Michael McCall quotes a college friend, Mike Woods, as describing Garth as a "polite womanizer." Mike said Garth and Sandy settled into monogamy rapidly. "He'd still talk about a girl being pretty or stuff like that, but as far as flirting, he just stopped it completely. He wouldn't have anything to do with other women after he met Sandy, not that I know about. He had always been the first one to make a move when we'd go out. But once Sandy came along, he was a changed man." Garth would change again when success went to his head, but that was in the future. . . .

Sandy's college friends couldn't understand what she saw in him. They argued he wasn't her type. Now, of course, everyone thinks Garth is the greatest thing since sliced bread. Sandy knows people "look at me and say, 'Why you?' I ask myself that also. My answer is, because I fell in love with a long-haired country boy long ago. I was there when it was, like, how many ways can we figure out how to cook potatoes?"

When it came time for him to make his big move in 1985, Garth expected to leave her behind forever. "I was a jerk. When I left, I didn't tell her, but I wasn't planning on coming back. I didn't think I'd see her again once I moved to Nashville." Later in his career he'd explain, "I thought I was emotionally prepared for a lot of stuff to happen, but I wasn't. If it hadn't been for a loving, determined wife, I would already be out of the business. Sandy is the driving force—she's as much Garth Brooks as I am."

After the first disappointing trip to Nashville Garth and Sandy were married, though Garth still wasn't convinced he was ready. "I hated being tied down . . . I was a spoiled ass. Responsibility, commitment, was not my game." He says he proposed to Sandy "because I thought she was so crazily in love with me, and that God had brought us together, that it had to be the right thing. Looking back, thank God I did. I realize there's no one better for me."

When asked why Sandy wanted to marry *him,* Garth giggles. "It has something to do with my physical build and good looks."

In 1987, a year after their wedding, Garth and Sandy took their nest egg of $1,500 out of the bank and set off for Nashville again. Garth says he might have given up all over again without Sandy to lean on. She gave him the courage to carry on, and sure enough, her gamble paid off.

If you poll a random sampling of male singers from any genre, nine out of ten will tell you they got into it for the women. Though rock and roll groupies get the most press, the antics of country music fans are equally bold. When Garth began touring in 1989, he found himself pelted with lingerie, flowers, and notes "about what they'd do if they got ahold of ya."

Success, when it came, brought a unique crop of problems, and the harvest was often bitter. Garth says, "I used to think, when I first got into this business, that Sandy was going to have to start doing everything I wanted her to, or I'd leave her in a minute. I thought, 'All of these women . . . I can have my choice.'"

Of course Sandy's far too spunky to be cowed by such Neanderthal antics. Garth says, "She's a little fireball, with a fiery temper, but she's a great woman who's every bit a lady. And she don't take nothing from nobody—'specially me."

Once Sandy even grabbed a woman who rushed the stage and gave her what for:

"When Sandy gets mad she counts to herself, and I can usually pick it up at about six or seven. One night this little gal was drunk and singing on the mike, trying to get as close to me as she could, and I looked out and Sandy was on three. . . .

I tried to figure out what to do, but she didn't even get to five. She just stood up and . . . Sandy grabbed her by the shoulder and threw her off the front of the stage and over the first table."

Sometimes Sandy rolled with the punches. Garth recalls the moment during his first Fan Fair appearance when a woman came up to the booth and gave him a pair of her panties to sign: "I thought, 'Oh, my God, this is it.' My wife just grabbed those panties . . .and put 'em on the table and spread the cotton crotch part of 'em out so I could sign 'em. I was amazed."

Still, Sandy draws the line at body parts, and who can blame her? "I was signing a lot of . . . uh . . . things," stammers Garth. "Sandy pointed that out. I took her out with me one night to Abilene, and that night blew the lid off everything. To start off, you sign articles of clothing, but as the night goes on you are signing articles of people. She sat me down, and even though she's a lot younger than me, she told me something about respect. She said, 'They would respect you more if you didn't do that . . . because you are married and you have a commitment to someone not to do that.'"

By his own admission Garth likes to "make love with my music in front of women. Ninety percent are fabulous looking, [but] the ones that scare me and my wife aren't the lookers in half T-shirts and nice ringers, who come to the bus askin' where you goin' later. It's the ones that know all the lyrics, who tell you how your music changed their life, how they played 'The Dance' at their husband's funeral. You almost fall in love because of how they feel."

Garth is fascinated by the opposite sex. "Women are so cool and as different as snowflakes. You can be with seven or eight women and get seven or eight sides of what a woman is. Women are neat, they're enticing."

Sadly, enticement proved too much for Garth's self-control. The whole phenomenon of instant success and nonstop touring kicked his already hyper side into warp 10. Before long he was burning his candle right up the middle! "I'll be honest with you, with it being the first time and the competition and all. I was going real wild. I'd have lasted maybe another year, year and a half at the rate I was going."

Garth played it fast and loose when he toured. He didn't call home for days at a time. He'd straggle home dog-tired, moody, and withdrawn. Though time together was terribly short, he and Sandy weren't communicating. Finally someone squealed. Sandy discovered her fears were true—Garth had been unfaithful. She was devastated. "I asked myself, why do I stay here? I know I love him, but . . ."

Writer Bob Millard points out, "In the beginning [Garth] approached [Sandy] in the typical macho way, paying more attention to how she fit into his plans than he did to who she was or what made her tick."

Garth now says, "Being true to someone carries a heavy weight on it. At the time I didn't think so. I thought, 'I love my wife to death, she's the only woman I could live with, so me messing around doesn't mean I love her any less.' Well, looking back now, that's bull. But at the time that's how I justified it."

On November 4, 1989, Sandy telephoned Garth before a show in Sikeston, Missouri."I told him my bags were packed, my plane tickets bought, and I'm gone. 'You come home and we'll talk, on my turf, eye to eye.'"

Doing the show after Sandy's call proved almost unendurable. Stillwater guitarist Ty England remembers how Garth choked with tears during the chorus of "If Tomorrow Never Comes," a song inspired by his love for Sandy. Ty said, "That night changed all our lives. We saw how much we could hurt somebody. Garth has said to me a million times that was probably the best thing that ever happened to him."

Scurrying home, Garth found Sandy poised for departure. "I wore out a pair of jeans in the knees, crawling behind her, trying to get her to stay. She told me, 'That's it. I'm gone.' Oh, man, I never cried so hard in my whole life, never begged so much. The day she told me she would come back is the day that I started to become the husband I needed to be."

Sandy definitely needed the upper hand in this do-or-die confrontation. Everything they believed in, all their wedding vows, their dreams for the future, were on the line. She told *People*, "I wanted Garth to feel my pain. He had hurt me so bad. I had wasted two years of my life is how I felt. I'd been the perfect little wife who thought everything was hunky-dory. The hardest thing was to keep from beating the holy shit outta Garth at the sight of him. He was ashamed, embarrassed, and it was written all over his face."

In 1992, Sandy told a reporter for *Life* magazine,

"If I'd known how big Garth was going to become, I don't know if I would have married him. All I've ever wanted was a white picket fence and kids — nothing more, nothing less — and I thought I was marrying the boy next door. We had to sit down and say, do we throw it all away or is there still love there? And we realized there was definitely still love, because neither of us could imagine the one without the other, even after all we'd gone through. And now that the baby's on the way, with the change that I've seen in Garth, I don't think we'll have too many problems,"

In retrospect, Sandy understands how they came to that low-water mark. This awareness doesn't dull the pain, only makes it more bearable. "Garth has always been a very sexual person. It was his ego: proving he could look out, point, and conquer. What made it easier to cope with was that it wasn't someone special. It didn't mean anything."

Garth's extremely thankful for Sandy's perseverance. He heeds Sandy's advice and credits her as the catalyst of his personal growth and newfound maturity. "Sandy's been the difference," he admits. " She sat me down and just said I needed to settle down—with or without her—because she wasn't going to sit around and watch me kill myself. So there's been a big change in me. I don't know if anybody sees it but me and her, but I'm happy to be me now. It takes a different breed to be an entertainer's spouse. If the shoe was on the other foot, I'd probably have left her a long time ago. . . . It took a helluva human being to forgive me."

For her part, Sandy says, "Garth kept showing me his love and that's what helped me the most, All these woman want him, but they can't have him. Now I look at it as a compliment."

In 1991, Sandy spent a lot of time on the road with Garth, which helped them both understand each other much better. It's tough to appreciate how grueling touring can be because on paper it sounds like such fun—visiting a different town every day, playing music all night and sleeping all day. Sandy said:

Garth saw me as someone who was . . . going to work in the morning, but at night . . . I could do anything I wanted to. He saw himself working constantly. . . . It came to the point where we were growing so far apart that we had to do something. That's when I quit my job and started going out on the road with him. . . . During those couple of days, it was enough for me to see what he did on the road. I felt real guilty then because I'd been thinking he'd been partying and he's been working just as hard, or harder, than I was.

To keep libidos in line, Garth and the band created a system of checks and balances—a vital backup since almost everyone is married. "I think the road could use a lot more gentlemen," says Garth. "When [the band] sees somebody falling a little bit, or leanin' in, the guys will get around and just talk to him. They ain't gonna say, 'Don't do this.' They're just going to say, 'Hey man, you need someone to talk to?'"

Garth says he now realizes there are certain thresholds that shouldn't be crossed:

There's a line you can go up to, and it's called the edge. . . . And a married man cannot dance at the edge, because sooner or later he's going to fall. So you gotta keep the edge away from you, and when it comes in sight, you really get scared.

You gotta keep remembering that at home you have stability and a love for eternity, someone that's believed in you from the start and cares enough about you to kill you, cares enough to fight and argue in this day when it's so easy to just say, "Let's go downtown and sign the papers and go our separate ways."

Bob Millard credits Garth with tremendous integrity. "It says a lot for Brooks and the sensitivity that drives his music that he continues to want to become more mature in that relationship, since life at the center of the singing-star hurricane is hardly the most conducive place to experience personal growth."

Sandy, too, has grown in this relationship. She discovered her own strength. "I was feeling much too sorry for [myself] because I wanted to lean on him, I wanted to be dependent. Finally, I said, 'To hell with that. I'm going to enjoy myself, do what I want to do, with or without him.' And I found someone inside who I had been hiding or running away from."

As for Garth, seeing Sandy on television during a TNN talk show finally helped him realize she's her own woman:

Now I was on the outside looking in, and it was a whole different perspective. It has always been difficult for me to be both a singer and a husband because I always thought they both demanded so much attention and that they were different things. So I just sat there and watched her talk. It wasn't so much what she said, but how she said it. I just watched her mouth move, and for once I was where I couldn't interrupt her and talk over her. I realized that this is not just Garth Brooks's wife, this is an individual human being. It gave me a whole new respect for her.

None of this means Garth wants temptations of the flesh to disappear entirely; after all, they're strong fuel for his muse. "Bleed it for all you've got and put it to music. That's a great way to write."

But they've mended their fences. In October of 1990, when Garth won the Country Music Association's Horizon award, he startled the live audience and TV viewers by dragging a reluctant Sandy up on-stage with him to accept it. "I'm not much good at it," he announced, "but when I don't sing, I try and be a husband. This is my wife, Sandy. I wouldn't come out without my right arm and my right leg, so why would I walk up without my wife?" Later, he explained, "We'd been holding hands all night, and to tell you the truth, it seemed more unnatural to leave her than to take her with me. She was very excited."

To celebrate their fifth wedding anniversary in May 1991, Garth rented an entire club in Nashville so they'd have some private time together. "It's my first date in about five years with my wife. We're gonna go dancin' like we used to." Afterward they had a private, romantic dinner.

Like Garth's music, this marriage is best classified as "new traditional," mixing old- and new-fashioned elements to create something that feels like a good fit. Both partners strive hard to make it work. Both are extremely candid with the press because Garth doesn't want to misrepresent himself to his fans, making himself out to be holier-than-thou when he's as human as the next fellow.

That candor carries over into their pillow talk, according to Garth. "There's some conversations I have with Sandy that I never ever thought I'd have with a wife. About fantasies, and the details of those fantasies, so we'll know exactly where we're coming from and what it's going to take to please each other."

This doesn't mean there aren't still fireworks. When Capitol Records threw a party honoring Garth's astounding #1 success with *Ropin' the Wind*, he revealed that he and Sandy fought over his video for "The Thunder Rolls"—the same video that drew fire from TNN and CMT. When discussing his concept for the controversial video, Sandy asked him not to film scenes where he made love to someone else or threatened to strike a child. *Both* were in the video and Sandy went ballistic. At the party he said, "I haven't done anything to deserve this woman, but I wouldn't be here without her support."

No doubt they made up their differences dramatically. Ever outspoken, Sandy told *People* magazine, "Garth loves to fight. He once said, 'There's an emotion that comes out in you that I never see until I get your blood goin'. I love that. Then I want to forget about it, take you in my arms, and make love to you all night long.' Now I know when Garth gets me riled up, he just wants to lay in the hay for a while. It's foreplay."

On the topic of their sex life, Garth stunned some people by announcing that infidelity improved their marriage!

Until recently I had the mentality, "Okay, if you don't want to put up with me, you can hit the road." She said, "Okay!" Then I finally straightened up. The wife I got back after my infidelity was fifteen times the woman I had. Like, "I'm gonna show you that anytime you leave this house, you're losing something."

I'm not telling anybody, "If you're not happy, go out and screw around because your wife will become a dynamo for you," but I got to be honest with you—that's what happened for me.

Garth says. "People want Sandy and me to be like Barbie and Ken, and we can't. I'm an average guy, Sandy's an average woman, and we have our troubles. What I did was very, very wrong. But at the same time I did it. Let me deal with it myself. I can't even say I won't make the same mistake again, because I don't know what tomorrow brings. But I do know I have the rest of my life to love my wife, and that's what I must do."

In autumn of 1991, Garth again surprised his fans when he said he'd be taking six months off to work on his marriage. "I gotta get to be a husband. I gotta get back to that. Sandy's had a hell of a lot of heartaches. She's got a lot of people telling her they could go to bed with her husband if they wanted to. It's bothering her."

From December 14, 1991, through June of 1992 he wouldn't tour. This would be his time to recharge the batteries, remember what it was like to live in a house instead of tour buses and hotels, and reconnect with his wife. Reality proved somewhat different.

"For every day I give Sandy, I turn around and give one or two to the music," he admitted in February of 1992. "This six months I'm taking off? It started out as six months for Sandy and me, and I bet you we won't have seven days in that six months."

Sandy countered, "He thinks he doesn't give me anything special. What he doesn't realize, it's those days when he calls his managers and says, 'Okay, today there's nothing [for business],' and he takes the whole day to do what I want to do. Those are the days I live for. I see a whole different man than the rest of the United States sees. . . . There will come a day in my life when it is just Garth and me. I might be seventy-five and toothless, but that's what keeps me going."

The Brookses weren't planning to have kids just yet, though Garth once said he'd like "as many as God will allow." In February of 1991 he said, "We're going to wait until our traveling shoes are worn-out—or at least don't fit anymore—then settle down and have some kids." Later that year he told a reporter he wasn't stable enough to be a dad: "My emotions run very quickly and very rapid and they're very hot. So with children, I lose patience very quickly. To be not stable enough means not being able to handle the responsibilities of a child and realize that a child is a living, growing being that's bound to make mistakes. I know that's sad to say, but I'm just being honest."

Well, nature has a way of surprising us. In July of 1992 Garth and Sandy welcomed Taylor Mayne Pearl. She's named Taylor because they like the name, Mayne because she was conceived in a cozy retreat in the Pine Tree state. Pearl pays homage to Minnie Pearl.

Colleen Brooks told *The Star* the pair stole off for a romantic, secret weekend at a quiet New England inn. "I guess each thought the other was doing something [about birth control], but they weren't." Colleen said, "This [baby] is going to wake Garth up in a lot of ways. It's a responsibility he was putting off." Parenthood brought out the more traditional side of their marriage. Sandy chose to stay home raising their family instead of working outside the home. Garth supports her in this:

Sandy's the kind of woman who says, "Wherever you go, I will follow." She likes for me to be the provider. She'd rather take care of the house and children. If people don't like that, all I can say is that they should do what's best for them, and I'll do what's best for me. I'm not going to put people down because they believe a husband and wife should both work and their kids should go to day care. If that's their way of doing it, best of luck and God bless them. The thing that works for me and Sandy is the old way, and that's the way we live our lives.

Yet Garth's not exactly the despotic lord and master. He told one Arizona reporter, "[She] tells me what to do. . . . I'm the boss around the house as long as my wife agrees with it."

Odds are high Garth and Sandy will make good, loving parents because they're so dedicated to one another and prepared to fight to preserve their union. "To say that we're through the hard times and the storm is over, I think would be very ignorant," predicts Garth. "Because my music is sexual, it always pushes those buttons. I will have to fight temptation from inside me for the rest of my life, as long as the music is there.

"I had to promise I'd make this marriage work. It ain't a bed of roses now, but we bust our asses, and it works unbelievably well. For the first time in my life, I feel good about being a husband and a partner. I love [Sandy] to death. When I've been down, Sandy has given me strength. That's definitely given me what I have."

Well, half a tux is better than none!
(photo: Ron Galella)

(photo: Mike Dubose)

Backstage at the awards, just three months before Taylor Mayne was born. (photo: London Features Int'l)

Smooching with Sandy behind the scenes.
(photo: Retna)

Sandy accompanying Garth to the 27th Annual Academy of Country Music Awards. (photo: Ron Galella)

Garth and Sandy celebrate their Oklahoma roots.
(photo: Retna)

(photo: Wide World)

“I’m not much good at it, but when I’m not performing, I try and be a good husband.”
(photo: Retna)

(photo: Peyton Hoge)

Chapter Five
Rich and Famous

No one could argue that 1989 wasn't a good year for Garth. But 1990 was *astounding!* As early as February he was telling reporters, "It's almost like a new being has been born. Suddenly I'm leading two lives. One life is the same as before, with my wife, Sandy. To her, I'm still 'Bear' and I'm her husband." Garth's other persona was an exuberant performer who chewed up stages careening from torchy balladeer to frenetic wild man in the space of a chord change.

Starting with the release of *Garth Brooks* in April of 1989, he and Stillwater spent most of the next eighteen months in motion, jolting adrenal glands into a hyperactive froth from coast to coast. That same year Garth grabbed a little downtime to write songs and complete his follow-up album, *No Fences*—no small feat considering the band's hectic schedule.

Garth gives tremendous thought to the content of his albums, and that means confronting his dueling sides and the pull between art and commerce. Here's a man who knows he has become merchandise. Interviewed in the *Lafayette* (La.) *Advertiser* in January, Garth said, "We love to take our time with an album. It's like selling a sandwich without any meat in it if you don't have a good one. I can only put out what I feel is worth the money. If this album isn't ready . . . we'll have to put it off until it is. I firmly believe in providing ten of the greatest songs you can find."

With his passion for meaningful lyrics and determination to pass on a message, Garth finds songwriting an intense experience, one he doesn't take lightly. "I won't write an idea unless it really hits me. A lot of guys write three hundred songs a year, pick about one in ten to record, and figure they're bound to hit with one in thirty. Not me."

Country tours differ from big rock tours because the performers frequently shuffle around and they play more dates. At the start of 1990, Garth was still dividing his time between opening and headlining at venues large and small. "Everybody switches around," he explained. "I'll be doing one show with Ricky Van Shelton between two Strait shows. It's a tossed salad. One night you're going to do your own thing in front of a few hundred people and the next night you're going to front somebody in front of ten thousand people, and the next night you do your own thing in front of six thousand. That's just how it is."

Before every show Garth and his band gather for a ritual. "I pick one guy. 'Do something that's going to shock me, something that's going to make me remember this night,'" he instructs. "And sure enough, they do." Then the band chants, "Remember, let's put the music and people first. One, two, three . . . it's *showtime!*"

Nervousness is natural before going onstage, but Garth is the rare performer who relishes his butterflies. "One of my favorite things about performing is how nervous I get before a show. When you've got to go out and fight against yourself—when you're so scared you've got to talk your knees into moving—it's a real high when you get on-stage and you've conquered the fear."

Asked which slot he'd rather fill, Garth humorously pointed out a certain "can't lose" feeling about opening. "In the opening slot . . . everybody comes to ignore you anyway. If you go out, put together a five-song set, and literally blow their socks off, it's just wonderful. If you

POLITICS

As another famous Oklahoman once said, "There ought to be a law against anybody going to Europe until they had seen the things we have in this country." Will Rogers would have approved of superpatriotic Garth Brooks. Asked where in the world he'd like to visit, Garth instantly replied, "The United States of America."

Writing in the *San Francisco Chronicle*, Edward Guthmann called Garth "an overwhelmingly sincere proponent of homespun American values." Garth loves John Wayne, his mom, and his flag. There's every reason to believe he loves apple pie, too, and hey, he drives a Chevrolet.

Garth's deepest-held values are worth noting should he ever run for public office:

> ***I think we've overshot paradise with a lot of things in life. And religion, patriotism, country music—I think we needed to stop while we were where we needed to be. To get the flag back out on the porch and God to the supper table.***
>
> ***The heroes I grew up on are gone. We need someone, maybe a bunch of someones, to say, "drugs are for losers and it's okay to drink, but it's not okay to get drunk."***
>
> ***I think it's important to realize who your artist is. You should know within five minutes what kind of person he is. My people know I couldn't carry a Christian's shoelace, but I know all my gifts come from the good Lord. Our shows talk about values and beliefs and at the same time show you that I'm no saint. I don't think I'm here to preach. I'm here to create music.***
>
> ***When I talk to children, I try to tell them things . . . anything from showing little boys how to shake hands, or how to tuck their shirt in nice. It's amazing how many children you meet that don't have fathers and mothers.***

Late in 1990 as tensions between the U.S. and Iraq escalated, Garth insisted he'd collect a uniform should war be declared. "[I'd enlist] as quick as I could get down there. . . . I'll take my stand and if it takes dying for that stand, that's what I'll do. I mean, that's the way I feel now. If the situation comes up I might run like hell, but right now I feel that way."

On another occasion, he said, "If it goes, I've got to go down and enlist and get out there. We're on the USO list and we actually got our shots and were ready to go entertain the guys when they canceled it. They said terrorist activity was real high."

When push came to actual shove, Garth didn't enlist nor did he "run like hell," though his manager Bob Doyle wound up in Saudi Arabia as a captain in the reserves. For his part, Garth opted to stay where he could do the most good, writing and performing music for our troops at home and abroad. Garth's music was included in an airlift of over two hundred thousand audiocassettes distributed to the armed forces in the Middle East. The project, called Operation Desert Song, was conceived of by Bob Doyle. He'd been sent a musical care package and decided it was just the thing to cheer up his fellow fighters.

go out and bomb, that's what they thought you would do. It's no pressure."

Garth's typical opening show consisted of a twenty-five-minute set, or roughly six songs. "Four off the first album and two songs we think will be singles off the new album."

Despite the audience response, Garth expressed bewilderment at his growing popularity. He'd ask himself, have all these people stumbled in by accident, looking for some other guy in a hat? "I always wonder if they aren't mistaking me for somebody else, but they seem to know all about me and about my songs."

As momentum escalated, Garth played fewer short sets. Sometimes he'd wind up starring when he'd been slated to open, and the other guy's name was still on the ticket. By August of 1990 a booking agent in Waco, Texas, said, "Garth has definitely outgrown the clubs in our market already; we're now looking at putting him in buildings from six thousand to seven thousand capacity. . . . He's an entertainer, not just a singer, and he'll never have a problem as a return act . . . not in Texas and Oklahoma and probably not anywhere."

Joe Faires, a promoter for Virginia's Bull Run Jamboree, praised Brooks's show lavishly: "[He] hits the stage with a grin the size of his cowboy hat. He thoroughly enjoys what he's doing, and it is so obvious in the way he relates to the audience and vice versa. Garth tugs at your heartstrings—a fabulous, natural entertainer. No one watching that guy could help but love him."

The switch to a ninety-minute headline act created its own set of difficulties for Garth and the band. They felt compelled to keep topping themselves. Being professionals, they rose to the challenge:

First, you were the underdog, and it didn't much matter what you'd do; people were nice to you. But now we're on a level where we have to go into a lot of places and turn around a crowd that maybe doesn't like you because you wear a hat. Or thinks, "Well, this guy's just a shadow of Clint Black."

So you go out there and start working and see 'em start to shift, and by the end of the show you're looking around, and your guitar player's screaming at you from ten feet away and you can only see his mouth moving; you can't hear nothin' except this crowd. That's when your heart gets to pumping so hard you take your guitar and throw it as hard as you can across the stage, and the crowd goes nuts.

Then you do something else to make 'em go nuts, and it starts passing back and forth, and you get more fired up than the crowd does. Then it gets into just total mania until finally it gets like sex: such a frustration and a big buildup and then it just finally blows out, the show's over, and you're sitting back on the bus going, "Holy cow! What just happened?"

Garth's naturally pretty bouncy, but he says his rowdy act was engineered to compensate for looking less handsome than his peers. The gorgeous George Straits of the world can stand still and croon, he's said, but guys like Garth have to whip it up, offering people something to look at besides a chubby, balding crooner in a ten-gallon hat.

Not surprisingly, this former marketing major looks into a crowd and automatically calculates the demographics. This helps him tailor the act. He told one reviewer: "At the clubs it's twenty-five [years old]. In concerts it's seventeen to nineteen years old." These breakdowns are important to Garth, who wants to set a good example for kids without appearing sanctimonious to their parents. Again referring to himself in the third person, Garth explains: "When I'm performing in a club and you know everyone is over twenty-one and it's packed wall to wall, this nut comes flying out and it's really interesting to see what he's going to do. Maybe five times in my career he's done something that wasn't that tasteful and we come back and apologize and go on with the show. It doesn't get that wild during the fair season. There's so much age variation in the audience."

Playing smaller venues is more to Garth's liking.

You can talk and get real personal. Sincerity is a big word for our show. The largest crowd we had as a headliner was right around seven thousand. It seemed like you were screaming into the night.

I love the personal things. The smaller crowds are nice because you can see each individual face and actually do a show for them. With the larger crowds—after about the first ten or fifteen rows—people's faces become just color and you can't make them out. You do your best, but you can't sing to someone who's half a mile away from you. So, I'm big on sincerity and big on very personal shows.

Yet as his television special two years later proved, Garth easily adapted himself to arena-size crowds. He found he has no problem making the stadium seem intimate. He connects with everyone—even fans unlucky enough to be sitting out in the ozone. That's because he takes the time to look and point and smile and wave. Garth hasn't forgotten his own concert-going years, when he desperately wanted to feel special, singled out.

I put myself out there and say, "What would I like?" What I would like is for some stolen moment in that concert when the artist looks at me. Then me and him or me and her have this moment, where I can tell him or her—this is how much I think of you. I've spent my hard-earned

PERFORMING VS. WRITING

It's easy to think of Garth Brooks as a split personality. There's strong, silent, moody Garth versus the loud exhibitionist of the concert stage. According to writer Michael McCall, Garth "works a crowd like a star linebacker or quarterback charging up a football team before a big game." This is the same guy who penned a love song while gazing at his sleeping wife. . . .

Most people are introverted or extroverted. Garth is both and accommodates a wide variety of fans whichever way he swings. "We have a saying. If you want to hear the CD note for note, stay home and listen to the CD. If you want to hear things a little out of tune, cranked and loud and a lot of fun, come out and give us a shot."

Garth considers himself an intense, tightly wound man who is equal parts dreamer and macho lout. "I take everything so seriosly. I even take taking out the garbage seriously," he admits.

If Garth had to pick one side and stay there, could he? That's a tough question, one he ponders frequently.

In 1990 he told *Music Row* magazine:

> *There are actually three [things] that make up what I do. There's recording, performing, and writing. I've gotta admit each one is the most wonderful in its own time.*
>
> *Since we've been touring so much, performing is probably the most natural thing that comes to me right now. Recording is like a bike, you have to get back into it. You remember how it's done and everything, but you're rusty. Songwriting scares me simply for the fact that I haven't written in probably over a year now because I haven't been mature enough to do both touring and writing at the same time.*

Garth believes strong material is paramount: "Your songs are your swords, your power. It's amazing the size of the sword you carry. I'm looking for beliefs . . . to let people know they aren't working for nothing, that what they see when they close their eyes at night doesn't always have to be a dream."

But he'd never be content limiting himself to writing:

> *A performer is a deliverer of a message . . . and I think that the song is very, very important, but entertaining is on the same importance level. They're not anywhere near the same thing. The same way writing songs and doing the studio work with them aren't the same thing. All are of equal value and all of them are as much fun to me as the other one. I think songwriting is so cool. It may be the most valuable to some because it's the birth of the thing. If you have crappy songs, your career is over. If you get a good list of singles underneath you, that separates the legends from the stars.*
>
> *There is an aura you step in on-stage, when the show is going on. You can see it all over yourself. You get the thumps, where your heart is louder than anything else. Little purple, squiggly lines get in your vision and everything starts to look like a negative. And you're just sitting there about to pass out, everything's spinning. It's almost to the point where you can stand there and say, "Shoot me, watch what happens."* Boom! *Nothing! I just want to go up there on that rope ladder, do a triple gainer, land on my head, get up, and just go do it again. . . . I'm in it for the power.*

He's in it for the rush. Sandy told reporters Garth has always been a sexual person, and he says a good show is, well . . .

> *A great concert is like great sex, where you get wild and frenzied, then turn that around quick to something gentle, tender, and slow, and then get wild and crazy again and just keep doing that over and over until one of you drops dead. It's the same great, physical thing with music, and it happens every night.*
>
> *On-stage is where my heart beats fastest and the wildest that my blood rushes. There's nothing like when the crowd is into it and you're just nailing it.*

Performing undoubtedly fulfills Garth's Aquarian need for lots and lots of friends. He makes thousands nightly! "You know, there's a feeling you get when there's only two people in the room. Well, I gotta be honest with you, there's been times when there's seventeen thousand people in the room—it's a lot better feeling than that."

money to be here, and my time most of all. And as an artist I can look at them and say, "Hey, this is how much I think of what you're doing for me. My dream is coming true because of you and I want to try and give something back to you."

It goes both ways. On good nights the crowd sends forth waves of electricity that can keep a performer tingling long after the last chorus has been sung. "As the audience gets wired up and crazy, we get more wired up and crazier . . . the adrenaline starts pumping and you just go nuts."

Houston Post pop critic Claudia Perry caught Garth's show in February of 1990 and reported that the crowd was responsive. Most knew the words to Garth's songs, and they spontaneously leapt to their feet to greet "If Tomorrow Never Comes." Around this time Garth's act included a hilarious spoof of Willie Nelson and Julio Iglesias's hit, "To All the Girls I've Loved." He sang both parts with over-the-top abandon.

Ultimately Perry was disappointed: "What rankled was the show seemed calculated." She missed the feeling that things could go wild, get out of hand. And she found Garth's modesty tough to swallow because he kept repeating, "Even if it all ends tomorrow, you're looking at the luckiest man on earth."

But Garth is *sincerely* having a blast, and he's thankful for it. From his perspective, performing is an endless recess, the stage his playground. "Mentally, man, I'm a kid. This is great . . . what a way to spend your day. . . . This ain't working.

"We throw guitars and scream at the audience, run out into the crowd, suddenly disappear offstage and appear somewhere standing on someone's table, kick beer bottles off tables, throw water at each other on stage and just have fun."

And Garth tells a great story about the time he blanked out, forgetting the words to his own hit, "Much Too Young." What's a superstar to do? "I just looked out in the crowd to see what they were singing and sang along!"

Robert Hilbrun, music critic for the *Los Angeles Times*, was blown away by Brooks's stage persona. "Advisory to rival country singers: Think twice before agreeing to follow Garth Brooks on-stage. . . . Put him on-stage . . . and he taps into the sociological currents of country music as well as anyone since the glory days of Willie and Waylon."

Jack Hurst, writing for the *Chicago Tribune*, noted Garth's "distinctive combination of smoulderingly intense masculinity, a tendency toward tears, a maverick flair for the unanticipated and a fierce determination to portray life in the raw."

Off stage, Garth impressed most interviewers with his shy, deferential, *polite* way. He has wonderful manners and answers questions thoughtfully. He's polite, shy, soft-spoken, and modest, but doesn't beat around the bush or prevaricate when asked even the most personal question. Garth calls people "ma'am" or "sir' — and not just his elders. One teenage record-store clerk working at Nashville's Rivergate Mall said Garth stopped off to see how his albums were selling and called her "ma'am" several times. "Listen dude, you don't have to call me 'ma'am,'" she teased—prompting a dig in the ribs from her store manager, who hissed, "Don't you know who that is?" "That's just how I was raised," came Garth's reply.

Reporters, amazed by his double-sided personality, call Garth the Dr. Jekyll and Mr. Hyde of country.

When not performing, Brooks rarely considers himself off-duty. His agent, Joe Harris, says, "Garth not only is a super entertainer on-stage, he does everything and more required offstage. The media, fans, and fair-board committees are delighted." At one Pennsylvania fair Garth signed autographs from ten-fifteen P.M. to one A.M. after giving a ninety-minute show in the rain.

Throughout the tour Garth made countless personal appearances, such as the one at a Louisiana Wal-Mart on January 19, 1990, where he signed autographs for hours. Why does he do it? "I get to see the people who are responsible for what I do face-to-face. That's a true pleasure for me."

Late in February, Garth dropped in on Wakefield Elementary School in Sherman, Texas, to read a story to Marci Conrad's kindergarten class as part of a special guest reader program. Marci's class had written Garth a letter and every student signed it. Though Garth lost Marci's phone number, he got a local deejay to track her down and put the wheels in motion. Garth showed up in his trademark striped shirt and cowboy hat. He was nervous. "[I've] never done anything like this program before." The kids were receptive and thoroughly enjoyed his reading of *The Barn Dance!* by Bill Martin, Jr., and John Archambault. Afterward Garth sang songs for the kids.

County fairs are a staple of a country performer's itinerary because they expose the singers to vast numbers of record buyers who might not have the time, money, or inclination to venture out to stadiums or honky-tonks. While enjoying a day out catching up on local farming achievements, playing games of chance, and taking turns on the rides, they also stop to listen to live music.

Garth says these fairs are "an intricate part of our foundation. . . . Around here, the arenas seat either forty to fifty people or ten thousand and we want to get to the people in between." County-fair ticket prices are generally low or even free, and the ambience is informal, personal.

So Garth missed most of the fair circuit in 1989 but overcompensated during the summer of 1990. To say that he's seen more of America than most campaigning politicians is no exaggeration. A random sampling of his bookings covers a lot of ground: Smyrna, Georgia; Hugo, Oklahoma; Carlinville, Illinois; Nacogdoches, Texas; Mexia, Texas; Saltville, Virginia; Myrtle Beach, South Carolina; South Bend, Indiana; Alpena, Michigan; Lebanon, Pennsylvania; Arkansas State Fair; Tyler, Texas; Tarleton State University in Texas; Boone County Fair, Iowa; Mount Pleasant, Texas; Shawano County, Wisconsin; Wyandotte County Fair, Kansas; Middle Tennessee District Fair.

That summer a writer for the *Ogden* (Iowa) *Reporter* asked Garth to describe a typical day on the road during a tour. The day starts at "the

OOPS!

Garth's not afraid to laugh at himself, especially if he knows he goofed. In 1990 Garth told a reporter for the *Marshfield* (Wisc.) *News-Herald* about this unrehearsed pratfall:

> ***My most embarrassing moment was when I was playing with Reba McEntire at a place called the Concord Pavilion on the West Coast. The whole stage was black, the floor and everything.***
>
> ***They didn't tell me there was an orchestra pit and it was open and I was out walking alone, waving to the people, singing. The next thing I knew, I had stepped right off into the pit and it scared me so much. No one could see me. I landed on my feet and I didn't miss a note because I was scared to death.***
>
> ***I hit the floor. I guess I was so pumped up and scared that I jumped right back up on the stage and everyone thought it was planned. I never was so scared in my life, because, when you're falling, you don't know whether it's one hundred feet or one hundred inches.***

A few months later Garth topped himself, though with less risk of personal injury. Performing at the American Royal Rodeo at Kemper Arena in Kansas City, Missouri, he stopped singing midsong when he spotted some men videotaping the show. Earlier, his people had announced a ban on video cameras.

Brian McTavish, reporting for the *Kansas City Star*, described the scene: "Then someone onstage pointed to the arena scoreboard. . . . Brooks finally realized that the cameras he was concerned about were being used to show his larger-than-life image to the audience on the scoreboard's four screens."

Garth apologized repeatedly. "I'm sorry that I made a fool of myself," he said, adding that it wasn't the first—or likely to be the last—time that happened! Ultimately his gaffe didn't matter, wrote McTavish. "Flashbulbs popped while calls of love showered on Brooks, whose likable personality and all-smiles demeanor won the day."

crack of noon," he joked. "Usually I wake up when we're thirty or forty minutes outside of the city where we're going or we're already parked in the parking lot."

He's awakened by Tim, the road manager, who briefs Garth about interviews, in-store appearances, and other commitments that will take up his day. "After that, I see all the other guys. There are eleven of us, and they tell me where they've been, what they've seen, and they mention the good places to eat and the places to stay away from."

Garth admitted that in-store appearances were a little unreal. "You start traveling without ever moving your feet. You just see so many people from so many different areas that it's neat . . . and the more you learn about people the more you can relate to them. It helps your songwriting and your performing."

Then it's time for dinner, often with staff from the local radio station, who want to talk shop about the records and the tour. This, too, is a learning experience. "You talk to them about how you can better your music, and they talk to you about how they can better their station." Garth sees deejays as his allies in the battle to get his music before the public, so he's glad to schmooze with them.

Once Garth's at the venue and the lights dim, "this guy pops out . . . and I don't know who he is, but he's just nuts. He loves to have fun. And he goes out there, and for ninty minutes, man, he just lives and breathes and jumps and hollers, screams, laughs, cries, does everything he can imagine, and when the show is over, he just kind of disappears and he'll wake up the next day."

After that it's back to reality. Like anyone coming home after a hard day's work, Garth changes out of his concert gear, climbs on board the bus, and plays some CDs to unwind. Depending on the schedule, the night will either be spent on the bus traveling to a new town or in a hotel catching some z's.

In the wee hours Garth stops the bus so he can call Sandy from a pay phone. She wakes up their Siberian husky, Sasha, for a quick woof with Dad.

Garth took part in the three-hour NBC special "Night of 100 Stars," which aired on May 21, 1990. He says the special, hosted by Jimmy Stewart, Helen Hayes, and Katherine Hepburn, was "really the night of ninty-nine stars and me."

Fate pushed the pedal to the metal beginning on Garth and Sandy's fourth anniversary, May 24, 1990. They'd been out shopping and returned to find a message that the album *Garth Brooks* had been certified gold. "Ever since that anniversary everything's been going wonderfully," Garth marvels. "It seems like I can fall off a ten-story building and land in a truck full of money."

In June, Garth appeared at Nashville's Fan Fair and stole the show. Fan Fair was created in the early seventies when hoards of devoted country listeners descended on the city one October to celebrate the Grand Ole Opry's birthday. Unable to handle the vast numbers, the music industry created Fan Fair to appease people eager to meet the stars. Held every June, the fair is a veritable convention consisting of performances and booths loaded with merchandise. Here fans can mingle with their favorite stars and get autographs and snapshots. It's a pay-one-price event that's limited to around 25,000 attendees. Tickets for 1992's festivities cost $75 and sold out well in advance of the June 8–14 dates.

When Garth performed, the crowd gave him a standing ovation for "If Tomorrow Never Comes." Capital president, Jimmy Bowen, came on-stage bearing a gold record. Garth wiped away a tear and said, "I'm going to present this to the people who truly gave it to me." With that, he walked to the front of the stage and held the record aloft, thanking the fans who had put it in his hands.

In July supersavvy Capitol released "The Dance" to radio stations on vinyl and CD singles. Heavy airplay pushed the song to #1, but fans couldn't buy it. Jimmy Bowen announced that he wasn't going to sell "The Dance" as a single because 65 percent of all singles return to the label unsold.

How clever! Fans who wanted "The Dance"

JIMMY BOWEN

No one's lukewarm about Jimmy Bowen, the controversial and colorful executive who took over as president of Capitol Nashville (now Liberty) in December of 1989. Bowen's outspoken, iconoclastic, and by all reports, tough to be around. Bowen is one of the industry's prime movers and he's had a major hand in shaping Garth Brooks's career.

In a 1990 *Journal of Country Music*, Bob Allen wrote: "Certainly, no one on the scene has been so persistently extolled and reviled, praised and damned, and so endlessly gossiped, speculated, and conjectured about as Bowen has."

Bowen was born in Santa Rita, New Mexico, and grew up in the Texas panhandle. For a brief moment in 1957 he had a hit with the song "Party Doll," but Bowen was savvy enough to know singing wasn't his forte. As a colleague put it when he heard Bowen singing recently, "He . . . makes Ricky Nelson sound like Caruso!"

Over the years Bowen's worked at virtually every end of the music business. He's been a singer and a disc jockey. He was a staff songwriter for American Music Company and wound up managing the company and producing their demos. In those days his roster of artists included such teen dreams as Fabian and Frankie Avalon.

He signed on as the A&R man for Sinatra's Reprise label and struck a mother lode producing Dean Martin in 1960s. Together they scored twenty-six hit singles, fifteen gold albums, and five platinum discs. Bowen worked the same magic for Old Blue Eyes, himself.

In 1974, Bowen surfaced as the head of MGM records. By 1976 he'd turned toward country music, embarking on a self-propelled tutorial that consisted of touring the Southern states by car, listening to local radio programs, attending barn dances, and talking with natives. On top of this he served a three-year apprenticeship at Glaser Brothers Studio, where he learned how country music is made.

Bowen was first hired by Joe Smith, now Liberty's senior West Coast executive, to head Elektra's Nashville operation in 1978. During that tenure Bowen signed Conway Twitty, the Bellamy Brothers, and Hank Williams, Jr. During the next fifteen years he'd head the Nashville divisions of MCA, Elecktra/Asylum, Warner Bros., MCA again, Universal Records (his own label), and Liberty.

Bowen's widely credited with moving country into the digital era. He's known for developing personal relationships with artists and encouraging them to become more involved in producing their own records.

He's a bulky, tall man who won't wear a tie ("I can't goddamn breathe in a tie"). He wears aviator glasses and sports a fisherman's cap. Bowen's brought a distinctly casual atmosphere to Music Row—but don't confuse casual with lazy. Whereas Bowen's addictive personality once manifested itself in an excess of alcohol and pot, nowadays he's a workaholic who even takes his cellular phone to the golf course, fielding calls between swings. He travels around Nashville in a customized chauffeured limo that's basically a mobile office. There's no downtime for this busy executive.

Bowen's been a powerful force in the careers of such superstars as George Strait, Reba McEntire, and Hank Williams, Jr. By his count Reba had sold roughly forty thousand per release when he began working with her, and he personally transformed the Oklahoma songbird into a household name. Whereas Strait moved about a quarter of a million copies of his albums pre-Bowen, afterward he went platinum. Just prior to joining Liberty, Bowen was running his own label, Universal Records, with such artists as Eddie Rabbit, Glen Campbell, and Hank Williams, Jr., under contract.

One reason Bowen's got so many enemies is because he tends to clean house, ruthlessly cutting both artist rosters and employees when he takes over a new label. According to some, he only does what's good for Jimmy Bowen. In his own defense, Bowen says Los Angeles never cared what he did, suggesting he has such a bad reputation in Nashville because it's essentially a small town where everyone gossips over the back fence. Allen notes,"It seems to give Bowen a sort of perverse glee that within Nashville's music industry, which devotes an almost ridiculous amount of time and expense to self-congratulatory, self-aggrandizing social rituals, his loner stance runs so resolutely against the grain."

By his own baffling description Bowen's a "Yankee" with a big mouth crashing through this small Southern city, speaking his mind whether they like it or not. He irritates people, but also inspires them. Reba McEntire said, "Jimmy's not wimpy, he's not wishy-washy. When he's on your side, he's on your side. If you bring him a song and it stinks, he'll tell you. If you do something he loves, he'll tell you. You always know where you stand with him."

Jim Fogelsong and Lynn Shults are the men who actually signed Garth Brooks to Liberty. By 1990, an informal guess suggested Brooks was responsible for 40 percent of the label's record sales that autumn. Allen writes, "It's interesting to consider where [Bowen] would be without Brooks. And he easily could have been, if he had relied on his own judgment, for when Bowen was last at MCA, Brooks had tried to land a deal with that label and was rejected. . . . Brooks was well on his way to a gold record before Bowen even arrived."

Whatever gossips said, Bowen had a powerful ally in Joe Smith, his once and future boss. Smith said he was thrilled to work with Jimmy again. "Bowen makes things happen. His successes at other labels are well known and we expect him to bring Capitol back to the prominence it once enjoyed in Nashville."

Garth was understandably nervous about the new deal. In November of 1990 he told *Music Row* magazine:

> *It was real scary, especially when everything you've heard about the guy . . . makes him a seven-headed dragon. . . . I distinctly remember telling him a month ago, "I've gotta be honest with you. You were a son of a bitch in my book according to everybody when you came here. You haven't lied to me yet. You haven't done anything but help me and my people." I must say I truly feel like a man on the end of a blessing with the emergence of Jimmy Bowen as a record man and Allen Reynolds as a producer. Because I think I get the true sincerity, heart and soul, in the grooves, and I think I get the aggressive dog-eat-dog marketing plan of probably the most successful record man that's ever been in the business.*

In another interview Garth expanded on this theme:

> *"I [told Bowen],'I love Allen Reynolds and I will stay with Allen Reynolds.' He said to me, 'You make the records with Allen, that's your job. My job is to sell 'em.' From day one, the man has been unbelievably sincere and honest, one of the greatest record men I've ever been involved with. . . . But I keep my eye on him,*
> same way he keeps his eye on me!"

Early in the relationship Bowen invited Garth to dinner and the two eyed each other warily. Neither knew what to expect or how to behave. Garth recalls:

> *I remember . . . I cut a piece of asparagus and it flew off my plate and off the table. Bowen's house has two servants and it's a real formal dining room and everything, and I just jumped down under the table and hopped down on my hands and knees to find it. Well, man, I wasn't really sure if he knew how to take that. My problem was the carpet was asparagus colored. I was down there a little longer than I wanted to be. . . . I think after that we both saw that we're both just human beings, and we both do—hate to call it one—but we do a job. . . . I hope he respects me as much as I respect him.*

Bowen had his own reservations—the advance word on Garth sounded like so much hype: "I've been in the business for thirty-six years. We're all skeptics. So when I met Garth, I thought, 'He can't be real.'" Watching Garth sign autographs for hours after a show transformed Bowen's attitude. He realized that fans believe in Garth "instantly. It's just amazing. I've never seen the response back to the stage like he has."

Rumors swirling around Nashville in the summer of 1992 suggest Bowen's on his way out at Liberty. If that should happen, he's bound to turn up somewhere equally advantageous—Bowen always lands on his feet. "I've never claimed to perform magic," he says. "My whole thing is to help artists do their music. I don't do it for them. . . . I think the nineties are going to be the most exciting era of country music. So I thought I might as well stick around and enjoy it. I thought I might as well ride the wave as long as I can, because it does knock you off at some point."

had to buy the entire CD. Bowen said, "I want them to buy the whole package, get involved with the whole artist. . . . Since 'The Dance' has been released, we've sold more than four hundred thousand copies of the album, so I know it's working."

Another example of Capital's marketing savvy is the practice of keeping Garth's ticket prices low, in the $15 range. "The less people pay at the gate, the more they'll spend inside. That's just simple logic," explains Garth. "I believe in the Wal-Mart school of business. The less people pay for a product that they are happy with, the happier they are with it. Our T-shirts are all one hundred percent cotton, about the heaviest weight you can buy. The shirt is an advertisement on someone's back. So we want to give people something that's going to last."

While the first album continued selling well, excitement about *No Fences* reached fever pitch. One Oklahoma radio station actually tricked Garth's mom into giving them a tape of "Friends in Low Places," then played the bootleg on the air. Airplay led to requests, requests to more airplay. Capitol wound up releasing the disc ahead of schedule. Writing in *The Tennessean*, critic Robert K. Oermann said, "This is the kind of thing that happens when rock stations are eager to jump the gun on new music by Bruce Springsteen or Michael Jackson, but it's practically unheard of in the country field."

Even Jimmy Bowen was impressed. "I know this kid is hot, but this is amazing! Leaks like this happened to me when I worked in pop music, but never in my career in country music have we had a situation like this."

Meanwhile the first album continued garnering accolades. "If Tomorrow Never Comes" won Song of the Year from the Nashville Songwriters Association. In August, it was voted Top International Single by readers of the U.K.-based magazine *Country Music People*.

Mid-August 1990 Garth performed at the Georgetown Fair in Illinois and spoke at length about the importance of these gigs:

I'll always need to be at square one. I have advanced past square one and I didn't like what I saw, so I came back. Past square one is where they treat you like a porcelain doll and you begin to expect it. You don't sign autographs and you don't do this and you don't do that. Square one is probably one of the greatest things for fairs today. It seems to me that they try to separate the fans and the artist so much. It's the fans and the good Lord that create the artist. You're one-on-one with the people at fairs.

As if to prove his point, Garth stuck around for hours after his concert signing autographs, posing for photographs, and talking to people.

Later that month he unexpectedly faced a fair crowd at Adrian, Michigan, solo because headliner Tanya Tucker was too ill to play. After sending her a get-well message from the stage, Garth said, "But the main purpose is to have a good time, and I hope we make you not regret it." Very few members of the capacity crowd requested refunds.

Garth joined a host of charity-minded musicians to play Farm Aid IV in Indianapolis, and fan that he is, he gushed, "It was quite a thrill to see myself on the same T-shirt as the great Jackson Browne."

In September the Country Music Association announced nominations for their annual awards. Newcomers dominated every category and Garth roped in five nominations. Hearing this, he remarked, "It's like getting five invitations to a dance and not knowing who you might get to dance with." His nominations were for Male Vocalist of the Year (along with Black, Rodney Crowell, Ricky Van Shelton, and George Strait); The Horizon Award, given to talented newcomers (the others were Alan Jackson, Kentucky Headhunters, Lorrie Morgan, and Travis Tritt); Single of the Year and Song of the Year for "If Tomorrow Never Comes"; and Video of the Year for "The Dance."

Garth's pretty philosophical about awards. He's competitive and likes winning, but doesn't overrate their importance. "If we win a couple it will be nice," he said about the 1990 CMA awards. "My career is not going to be made or lost because of that. I'm back to the fans. I love them. I want them to love what I have to offer."

In the face of such recognition, would Garth get smug? Doubtful. He takes the phrase *self-affacing* to new extremes. "I think maybe in twenty years or maybe when it's the last day of my life, I can look back and say, 'I made it through the door. I did make it.' I've had very fortunate luck with the charts, and I'm still not 'in' to me." Aw shucks, Garth!

Captured in concert. (photo: Retna)

(photo: Nina Alexandrenka)

(photo: Peyton Hoge)

(photo: Peyton Hoge)

(photo: Peyton Hoge)

(photo: Peyton Hoge)

(photo: Peyton Hoge)

Sign of the changing times? Life christens Garth a pop star.

RTH BROOKS

erica's Hottest
Star Talks About
, Love and Fame

Garth's grin sells magazines—from the ridiculous to the sublime.

Lose 20 lbs. for spring
...on easy new microwave diet
NATIONAL ENQUIRER
Over 100 features every week
LIZ BIRTHDAY PHOTOS
Why Michael Jackson was a no-show at her 60th
GARTH BROOKS SURPRISING CHILDHOOD
• He hated country music
• His lesbian sister saved him from bullies
• He was a flop with girls
Garth at age 11
New rape nightmare for TV news anchor
COSBY EXCLUSIVE
My final show – how it all ends
'Beverly Hills' hunks risk their lives in 200-ft. bungee jump
PREDICTIONS
ROMANCES WEDDINGS BABIES & DIVORCES
...what's in store for your favorite stars
NATIONAL Examiner
The story every parent must read
A CHILD MOLESTER CONFESSES
GARTH
THE NEW WOMAN IN HIS LIFE
LUCCI
Why she can't survive without Jack
CHILI PEPPERS BRING RELIEF FOR ALLERGY SUFFERERS
AWARDS

Jamming with the band. (photo: Retna)

Garth thanks his fans for his award.
(photo: Wide World)

A broody pose from the man critics call country's Dr. Jekyl and Mr. Hyde.

This poster spotlights Garth's trademark look—
jeans, black Stetson, and a color-splashed shirt.

Posters like this are hot sellers along Nashville's Music Row.

(photo: Nina Alexandrenka)

(photo: Nina Alexandrenka)

This is starting to be a familiar pose. (photo: Retna)

Critics argue he's more pop than country, but these publications tell a different story.

(photo: Peyton Hoge)

Chapter Six
No Fences

Garth's second album, *No Fences,* shipped gold and boasted a top-ten hit—"Friends in Low Places"—before it went on sale in September 1990! Almost immediately the album shot past releases by Bon Jovi, Prince, and Raitt to land at #1.

Though Garth only cowrote four of its tunes, he feels *No Fences* represents him better than *Garth Brooks*, which he terms a "really innocent album." Sheer exhaustion enabled Garth to lighten up in the recording studio. "With that first album, Allen told me to loosen up, be myself, and I couldn't because I was so scared. This second album, I was so tired from touring, I was just myself. . . . Allen said, 'That's the sound I've been looking for.' When Bowen heard it, he said it was the greatest piece of product he'd heard since he's been in Nashville."

Garth had tremendous fun picking material for *No Fences*:

I get a kick out of listening to tapes. It's like Christmas—you get to open all this stuff you haven't heard before. It's a little sad because with every tape you're hoping it's a smash, and most of them aren't that good, but there are a lot of good songs out there. [Producer] Jerry Kennedy told me, "The one song you don't listen to is the smash hit you needed." I take that seriously.

The whole album's different. . . . Once we looked at it and what had gone on, it was like . . . how in the world can you label this thing or box it? We've got ten extremely different cuts on it, and the major objective of it is we've gained a lot of fans and friends with the first album and we just don't want to let any of them down with the second one.

Reviewing the album for the *Los Angeles Times*, Randy Lewis called it "[a] considerable improvement artistically, but more because of the weaknesses of the first—which sank musically under the weight of one hopelessly melodramatic song after another—than because of the modest yields of the second." He had praise, however, for Brooks's "woody baritone."

Stereo Review called it "different, varied and entertaining enough to distance Brooks from almost any other competitor. By next year's awards," they correctly predicted, "Brooks will probably have them shaking in their boots."

The *Washington Post*'s Mike Joyce said Garth's powerful voice verges on "sounding like honky-tonk parody—all warble and tears. . . . He's the sort of singer who can divide the word 'cry' into half a dozen syllables."

Perhaps the funniest—and most quoted—review came from Ken Tucker in New York's *Village Voice*. Tucker said, "With his eerily calm demeanor and face like a thumb with a hat on it, Garth Brooks is the sort of country singer that David Lynch might have created."

Tucker points out that Garth and his fellow New Traditionalists aren't the first country artists to jump the fence between pop and country. He cites precedents set by Willie Nelson's *Stardust* album and the collaboration *Trio*, from Linda Ronstat, Dolly Parton, and Emmylou Harris.

While Tucker can't resist dubbing him the "singing thumb," he praises Garth's "deadpan irony" on "Friends," and his ability to begin the chorus high then drop his voice on the word *low*, a technical achievement not every singer can master.

Country Music found the second album "full

of the same gentility, faith, optimism, Western smoothness and sophistication that have made his style of neo-country such a big hit with listeners. . . . As *No Fences* amply demonstrates, he's sure got the talent, conviction and finesse to back himself up, no matter what his next move is."

Garth's monster hit "Friends in Low Places" was penned by Bud Lee and Dewayne Blackwell. Blackwell also wrote "Mr. Blue," a 1950s hit for the Fleetwoods, which Garth cut on this album. "Friends," with its escalating chorus for a cast of thousands, is the ultimate party song. It's playful and rowdy and a staple on barroom jukeboxes nowadays. As Garth himself says, "We've had a lot of fun with that song, but it's nothing to base your values on."

Unbelievably, Garth almost missed out on the biggest song of his career. Due to a misunderstanding, Mark Chesnutt recorded "Friends" before Garth did, but Garth tied up licensing rights so only he could release it as a single.

We didn't cut the song in the first three tracks off the album, because at the time we were doing serious ballads. Dewayne panicked and figured I wouldn't cut it. So he sent it out again. Chesnutt picked it up, put it on his album, and I went through the roof! I'd been playing it a year in my live shows. I went and got the restraining license where only I could have it as a single. I'm not sure if it was a great move for Chesnutt to keep it on his album. His cut was very down and I think it hurt him badly 'cause every place I was goin', people were playing the cuts back-to-back."

Garth adds, "The appeal of 'Friends,' I think, is that the character is such an underdog, so much like me, so much like everybody. I think that's what people like about it."

Garth hasn't written songs with Blackwell because he's suffering from a bad case of hero worship. "I'm so in awe of him, I don't give him an honest opinion. . . . To me, he's an all-or-nothing guy. He either writes a song that knocks me out of my shoes or it don't get close."

Blackwell says most listeners think the song's about a man who crashes his ex's wedding, "but it wasn't really a wedding. My wife is from a wealthy family, and it really came out of a formal affair. I showed up at a Thanksgiving dinner like a typical songwriter—not dressed for the occasion and a little tipped—and the song was based around that."

"Unanswered Prayers" tells the story of a married man who encounters his high school sweetheart and thanks God they didn't wind up together. Garth linked its theme to his first Nashville visit. "It's not only a thing about love. It's a thing about all the things we wish for, where we think we can step in and write in what the good Lord wants us to do. It's nothing that's wrong in my book. It's. . . . very normal because we're all trying to find our purpose."

He cut another song by Tony Arata called "Same Old Story" and joked about Tony's career prospects: "It's like anything that's good . . . once you find anybody that you can groove with real well, you go back to the well as many times as you can. I was telling Tony . . . 'For your sake I hope you get everything that's coming to you, and for my sake I hope nobody gives you the time of day.' I think he's wonderful. He's an unbelievable well that's never been tapped."

"The Thunder Rolls," a moody tune about infidelity, comes from Garth and Pat Alger, a songwriter Allen Reynolds fixed Garth up with. Garth resisted his producer's matchmaking, but in the end found Alger a terrific guy, "very honest. Didn't care if he was gonna upset anybody 'cause he's gonna tell you his opinion. Which made me love him right off 'cause those kind of people are few and far between in Nashville."

Of the story behind the sad song "Wolves," Garth said, "The farm was used just as a thing to draw a picture, not to take literally. . . . It's about homelessness, it's you and me, it's everybody that tried to keep ahead of the debt ball, to keep from being rolled over."

He cowrote "New Way to Fly" with Kim Williams, a writer who's had great success in Nashville. That's another match that almost wasn't struck. At first Garth was reluctant to hook up with Williams. He liked—not loved—the Williams songs he was hearing, and heard that the author was disfigured. Garth's a little

DO CLOTHES MAKE THE MAN?

When you hear the words *country singer*, what sartorial image flashes through your mind? Pointy, neon-hued boots emblazoned with fancy scrollwork and the singer's name? The man in black? Sky-high blond wigs, inch-thick makeup, rhinestone studs and stilettos? Embroidered lime-green tuxedos?

Well, country's changed. While sequins will always have a home in Nashville, New Traditionalists such as Garth Brooks have a distinctive look. Their uniform consists of a hat, clean shirt, optional vest, new (unripped) jeans, boots, and an acoustic guitar strapped across the chest. How can you achieve the Garth Brooks look? You'll need these basics:

Shirt

Originally, Garth favored vertically striped shirts because they made him look thinner. The tall Oklahoman's stocky and his weight fluctuates; he's gone as high as 225, but he's happier around 198. Either way, stripes stuck. "All the gifts I got were stripes," he explained.

Stripes aren't mandatory, though. In 1992, Garth told *USA Weekend*, "Any kind of shirt will do, as long as it makes the statement, 'Hey, I'm screaming to be unique.'"

Lately Garth's been buying shirts from cowboy Maury Tate. This twenty-five-year-old Oklahoma native (born in Apache) was the 1991 champion calf roper at the Dodge National Circuit Finals, but he's gaining more fame for the flashy shirts he designs and sells under the Mo Betta label, priced around $85. Garth's crazy about these brightly patterned shirts. "I know that if I've got one of Maury's shirts on, there's a slim chance that someone else is going to have it on, too. I love Maury's shirts because I don't think he makes more than three or four of a kind."

Hat

They don't call him a hat act for nothing! "Garth Brooks is doing for cowboy hats what Indiana Jones did for fedoras," says Tom Pyle of J.J. Hat Center in Manhattan. John Rosenthal, general manager for Stetson, adds, "Garth's style is original. He wears several hats, but he shapes them distinctively."

Bob Posey of Resistol Hats says Garth's are "typical of hats worn by a certain part of the young rodeo crowd." Garth's hat has eyelets on the side, and it's worn at a rakish tilt with the back brim turned down, and the crease at the crown sloped forward. Garth has been spotted in gray, black, and white hats. They retail between $100 and $200.

Boots

Garth and other country performers prefer boots called Ropers. Unlike the pointy-toed cowboy boots familiar to most urban dudes, these have wide, round toes, low heels, and shoelike soles. Garth calls them "a cowboy tennis shoe." His favorites are Elephant Ropers, a line that's been discontinued by Justin Boots of Fort Worth, Texas. As a result, Garth keeps his eyes open for the boots when touring, buying as many pairs as he can find in local shops.

Jeans

Whether they're black or acid-washed blue, Garth's partial to Wrangler jeans. Why? "They fit. There's not much style in Oklahoma. There's mostly Wranglers."

squeamish. "They told me he had been in an accident and half his face was pretty much gone. I don't handle those things very well. But he's such a lovable man. He made a joke one time: we were talking about Lyle Lovett and he said, 'Hell, I'm better looking than Lovett and I've been on fire!'"

In October 1990, Oklahoma governor Henry Bellmon gave Garth a special award for promoting a positive image of his home state. October also marked Garth's induction into the Grand Ole Opry cast during the week of festivities celebrating its sixty-fifth anniversary. The induction was broadcast live during the seven-thirty show. Garth enthused, "I've always been treated like family when I was at the Opry. But now to be recognized among the class of honors that will never be topped, no matter how long or how far my career goes . . . This is the big one."

Speaking on behalf of the Opry, general manager Hal Durham said, "We think he is one

[See box page 124]

In 1990, Garth also debuted on the "Tonight Show" with Jay Leno. Another guest that night was Craig T. Nelson from the hit ABC series "Coach." Nelson impressed the hell out of Garth when he stopped by his dressing room to say howdy. "He came to my room and I thought to myself, 'This is the dad from *Poltergeist* and he's talking to me,'" gushed Garth.

In November, Garth rode the turkey float during Macy's annual Thanksgiving Day parade in Manhattan. He also played a show in Lincoln, Nebraska, and rocked the house down. The *Journal* said, "Lincoln got a lesson in prairie-fire popularity Thursday night courtesy of Garth Brooks. . . . [He] had the emotion and vitality of a great soul singer. . . . That looseness, genuine pleasure and enthusiasm is a welcome sight in country whose sober new traditionalists have gotten a little stodgy of late."

December found Garth playing around southern California. On the ninth he hosted an hour-long special called "A Country Christmas Tapestry" for radio airing on December 14, 15, and 16. Brooks's cohosts were Tanya Tucker, Gary Morris, and Larry Gatlin. The quartet reminisced about childhood Christmases, sang their own works, and introduced other performers.

Busy as he is, Garth's never one to ignore a friend in need—and everyone is a potential friend in his book. Newspapers are full of Garth Brooks "rescue" stories because he's the first to pitch in and help if someone's having problems. Around this time the *Oklahoman* reported on poor Birdie Wilton, who got a flat tire while driving down Interstate 40 one rainy night. She lit flares and waited for three hours, but no one stopped to help her. That is, until two big buses pulled over and a bunch of young men came bustling to her assistance. While they were fixing Birdie's tire, they sent her onto the lead bus to warm up—and meet Garth!

On December 17, Garth played a benefit at his old high school auditorium to raise money for the Future Farmers of America. Mayor Jim Blankenship proclaimed the seventeenth Garth Brooks Day.

Why did Garth work so hard in 1990? Believe it or not, he started out "scared to death I wouldn't have any work," so he took every job he was offered! It's hard to imagine he'd be so insecure, given his success, but that's just part of the enduring paradox of his complex personality.

Once, after working fifty-two days in a row, Garth wandered in looking so haggard and beat-up that it terrified his mom. "I looked like hell," he said, "and my voice was gone and my hair was almost totally gray on the sides. She was worried to death and I remember leaving a note by the breadbox . . . that said, 'Mom, if this kills me, I'll die happy.'"

Life could be arranged so it would be marginally easier, but Garth doesn't flex his star-power and fly to gigs while the band and crew burn up the highways. In fact Garth generally takes a turn driving the tour bus. Why? "I can't separate myself from my people. . . . And I'd love to be with my wife more, and flying would allow me to, but I love my people. This is how I know what they're thinking and what's going on."

Winding down the year, he predicted a slower 1991. "We're going to look at booking a little more realistically and try to keep it down to one hundred or one hundred and fifty dates," he said, adding, "I think your success in touring depends on who you're married to, and you're married to a crew. . . . We get along great. They support me and they work hard so I don't have to. So the touring doesn't really hurt, it's just that I think we've done a little too much of it this summer simply because we have people who have wives and children and they need to get back."

Garth knows the debt he owes this supporting team. "I also think that you're only as good as the people you surround yourself with, and I feel that I've surrounded myself with the people that will take me where I want to be and that's the best that I can be."

Besides his band, Stillwater, Garth's backed by the new regime at Capitol, which changed dramatically with the ejection of Lynn Shults and Jim Fogelsong and the entrance of Jimmy Bowen and his people. "I feel like we went from a label that was just surviving to a label that actually took the offensive, and—I miss the old family, I love them to death—but this new family is definitely a record-selling bunch of people."

On another occasion Garth admitted it's handy having others who can do his dirty work. He gave this garbled quote to *Music Row* magazine in November 1990: "The more people that you take over or pass, supposedly the better off you are. The industry is like that. I have people that do that side. And that's what I've gotta remember. There are people there because I had faith enough in them to put them there, and as far as Capitol Records goes, they know their stuff, and you've just gotta say, 'Hey, I've gotta handle this end of it.' And they handle that end of it and stay out of it."

With Garth poised to take over the nineties, manager Pam Lewis said, "If we need a name for what we're doing, we could call it 'melting pot management.' Garth, Bob, and I are a team. We all bring different skills and different perspectives. . . . I honestly feel we're making history here, and that's my second time to do that. I was on the original team of MTV, right in the middle of all that young, innovative energy. . . . This time we're on the way to Garth Brooks becoming a legend, and I'm loving every minute of it!"

Garth predicted great things for country. "I really believe that country music is in for a big change in the 1990s. I'm willing to take that big step, and if I fall, then so be it."

You'll rarely catch Garth wearing the whole tuxedo!
(photo: London Features Int'l)

Offstage, Garth favors comfortable workout clothes.
(photo: Ron Galella)

Hamming it up with his band Stillwater.
(photo: Retna)

Takamine

At an early concert, in a trademark striped shirt.
(photo: London Features Int'l)

He's at home on stage.
(photo: London Features Int'l)

(photo: London Features Int'l)

Aw shucks . . .

At the Macy's Thanksgiving Parade in Manhattan.
(photo: Retna)

Garth's an intense performer. (photo: London Features Int'l)

Making sweet music.

Once again, Garth dresses up—and down!
(photo: Retna)

Chapter Eight
Ropin' Stardom

Garth made the history books in September 1991 when he became the first country performer to *debut* at #1 on *Billboard's* Top 200 album chart. *Ropin' the Wind* shipped double platinum, thanks, once again, to Capitol's remarkable marketing tactics. Joe Mansfield, the label's vice president of sales and marketing, said, "The attack here is going to be for four pieces of product." This included the three albums and a video compilation. "All of our advertising encompasses all of [the product]. For every major account, we've bought everything available from September through December." In addition, retailers got plenty of backup materials such as posters, mobiles, and stand-up figures that they could use to create displays. And getting a special display devoted to your artist is tantamount to buying real estate in the store.

Well, all right. But what *about* the product?

Garth describes *Ropin' the Wind* as a "postcards-from-the-edge album—every song is pretty much out there on the limb. I've only got a few songs that to me are standards." He told the *Nashville Banner*, "We're taking some lefts and some rights. Trying some new stuff and keeping some old stuff. Basically, we're trying to do what we do every album, and that's make it worth the money that these people spend to buy it."

Initially Garth was tense heading into the studio, but producer Allen Reynolds calmed his fears. "Allen said, 'This third album will do what it's supposed to do,' and just with those words I felt real calm and relaxed and the whole thing fell together just like *No Fences* did." Like the first two albums, *Ropin'* was made for about $100,000.

The first single off *Ropin'* was "Rodeo," a song Garth described as "more like an old Creedence Clearwater tune. I don't know if I've heard a rodeo song that has this kind of beat or funk to it."

Many were apalled that Garth covered Billy Joel's "Shameless," and he defended himself admirably. After all, I'm only giving the people what they want, he argued. "What convinced me to do [it] was we play it live and the crowd is just loving it. At the fan club meetings we have after the shows, they're bringing it up every meeting. That's the same thing I got with 'Friends in Low Places.'"

And, naturally, Garth loved the lyrics: "The lyric is something that me as a spouse would love to hear my mate say to me. The people that actually get it, that understand what's going on with 'Shameless,' the first thing they come up to me and say, 'My God, what a lyric. What a way to say what he's saying.' That makes me feel good. . . . It's not a pop song written by a rock act. It's a song done entirely for the lyric, not as much for the performance."

Garth had his work cut out convincing Allen Reynolds, who admitted he "was probably a little more confused about it than [Garth] was. . . . But by the time he spoke of recording it, he had . . . already been getting enormous feedback."

According to Brooks, Joel's tune sends the message "I'd crawl ten yards through broken glass on my hands and knees just for you to kick me in the face." Garth has loved the song since its appearance on Billy Joel's *Stormfront* album, and he watched to see whether Joel would release it as a single before "moving on it."

Victoria Shaw's song, "The River," is "about

dreamers and about going for what you believe in." From here on in this song replaced "The Dance" as the final tune in concert.

Garth's gone on record saying he limits himself to five compositions (or cocompositions) per album, but he contributed seven to *Ropin'* because "these just seemed to fit the mood that I was in during the whole album's creation." He worries, though, that other writers will "give up on him" and stresses that his quest for good songs is ongoing.

Reviews for this new album were mixed. *L.A. Times* critic Robert Hilbrun gave it two and a half out of a possible five stars and asked rhetorically how Brooks had gotten so big with so few good songs per album. The answer, he said, is his live show. "Brooks delivers his most affecting songs on-stage with a genuineness and good ol' boy exuberance that touches you in the same warm, uplifting way that, say, Bruce Springsteen does in rock."

Hilbrun took Garth to task for choosing poor material. That's a sore point, since Garth views his songs as a source of particular pride. Hilbrun felt the young singer evinces "an apparent inability to resist story songs—even if the stories are old . . . old . . . old."

Garth would argue that he speaks to people's fundamental humanity—and that's old as the hills. He doesn't choose songs willy-nilly. "The one thing that can keep you out there today is the material. As long as the material is there, hopefully the artist will be there. If the artist is a jerk, material isn't going to make any difference; but if you treat people the way they want to be treated, it's the material that will make the difference."

It's worth noting that producer Allen Reynolds has tremendous sway in deciding what makes it to the disc. Garth won't release songs Reynolds doesn't approve of, regardless of their authorship. For *Ropin'*, Reynolds said, "We looked and listened widely to thousands of tapes and never found anything that would knock two of his off the list. . . . He's not one of these big, raging egos. He wants to do good work. I've said this to a lot of people: that the guy's talent obviously impresses me . . . but his character impresses me equally, if not more. . . . I've never worked with anyone who was this fully formed when I met them, in terms of their artistic maturity and sense of self."

Claudia Perry, reviewing the album in the *Houston Post*, said the "latest may be best." She decided Garth's astounding popularity didn't negate talent as is usually the case. Then she dubbed Garth "the Pillsbury Dough Boy of Young Country Hunks." Ouch! Though she praised *Ropin'* more than she damned it, Perry was one of those who disdained Garth's material. Around the time of his NBC special the following year, she'd write, "Let's just say some have a hard time believing that recording a song by pop's grizzled monument to mediocrity, Billy Joel, constitutes a serious risk."

A truly bad review came from *Rolling Stone*, which called Garth "the Vanilla Ice of country music, a million seller with a K Mart take on C&W tradition." The reviewer saw no wit, artistry, or authenticity in Brooks's product.

Let's hope Garth didn't read *that*, since he gets worked up over bad reviews. "It's something that kills me. I really believe you *can* please everybody all the time, if you try hard enough."

Stereo Review, on the other hand, gave Garth full points for authenticity. "No cardboard-cutout singer could have created 'Papa Loved Mama,' a terrific novelty tune inspired by a poem by Carl Sandburg . . . which Brooks expands into the biography of a jealous trucker and his cuckolding wife."

Us offered guarded praise. "Given some time, the jagged little crack in Brooks's voice deepens each one of [his] simple metaphors and familiar images. . . . The bulk of *Ropin' the Wind* quietly suggests that Brooks is growing into his role as a modern honky-tonker and is even getting better at it."

Music Row said, "A fine line separates Garth Brooks from Nashville's formula junkies. It's not that Brooks is the best looking, the best writer, or the best singer, though he's exceptional in all these areas. The difference is this: Garth works the formulas, while the others let the formulas work them."

Geoffry Himes, in the *Washington Post*, speculated that *Billboard*'s new country-heavy charts were just a belated reflection of what's always been true, rather than an indication that country music was suddenly taking over the universe. He felt much of this album was rock and roll in everything but name. "Brooks handles these untamed-male anthems well, belting out their boasts in his appealing tenor [sic] as if there wasn't a doubt in his mind about what he was singing."

That certainty is also Brooks's downfall, he said, because it limits his emotions to black and white without any subtle grays. He praised Garth's sincerity on the ballads: "Just as he focuses only on the positive in his up-tempo numbers, he focuses only on the negative in these slow laments."

That assessment was echoed by Andrew McLenon, copresident of Zoo/Praxis International records. After seeing Garth in concert he noted, "Every line in his ballads seemed like a life-or-death situation when he was putting them across." He easily spotted Garth's debt to rock and roll. "Every time he would even strum his guitar, the body English was totally rock and roll. I don't think it has ever been done in country like this."

In *Country Music* Patrick Carr devoted several columns to Brooks's new release, asking, "By what standards should we measure Garth Brooks?" Should the album be considered in light of Garth's possible socio-musical importance or should it be considered purely in terms of its unadorned merit as a collection of music?

Carr found nothing on the new release that struck him as much as Garth's earlier work and took him to task for relying on hackneyed clichés and outdated images. He concluded that the songs were clever, but offered nothing new or unique. Perhaps they're *too* slick, he suggested, adding that Garth only gave "the illusion of depth. . . . Here is an artist who can dress up some pretty modest visions with some awfully ardent brushwork."

Nevertheless, Carr gushed over Garth's voice. "Any singer who can move you as gently as Don McLean, Western-swing you almost as well as Merle Haggard and pump up big-hall emotionalism approaching Elton John's, all on one disc, is doing okay and then some."

The *New York Times* dubbed Garth the Kevin Costner of country music and harped on his meat-and-potatoes image and "goony grin." They decided Garth's fans consist of aging boomers for whom "country radio has become a sanctuary, a place where familiar old genres are reborn."

But let's get back to those album sales. Astounding! The music buyer for Ernest Tubb Record Shops gushed, "What's the expression? It's blowing out the roof. Our store in Pigeon Forge sold out the first day. We've sold something like two hundred cassettes."

Just after the release of *Ropin'*, Lew Garrett, vice president of sales for the Camelot record chain, said, "If it weren't for the Guns 'n' Roses project, [Garth's] record would have been the story of the year. We've already sold sixty thousand copies out of the one hundred thousand we ordered and we've reordered another twenty-five thousand. . . . Brooks is a pop mainstream artist, unquestionably a monster act."

CEMA Distributors, a wholesaler that supplies retail outlets, sold 1.7 million units prior to the album's release and needed 900,000 more the following week. The Sound Warehouse store in Tulsa had to open at seven-thirty A.M. to deal with fans and sold 750 albums by nine A.M. All told, the eight Sound Warehouse stores in Oklahoma accounted for more than three thousand sales that first day. Fans in Sacramento, California, lined up outside a store before it opened. A line of eager Houston buyers stretched for three blocks. The Tower store in Campbell, California, also opened early and featured a live remote radio show. Within ninety minutes they'd sold three hundred copies of *Ropin'*.

Mike Fine of Soundscan put it succinctly: "From Florida to California, Garth Brooks rules."

Garth's people were delirious. Jimmy

Bowen crowed, "I got into this business in 1956, and this is the first time since Elvis Presley that I've seen a solo entertainer have this kind of impact. He's selling out everywhere."

"Whoopee," squealed Pam Lewis. "The projections are that he's going to continue to sell away. They're saying this album will sell ten million copies!"

On September 24 the Country Music Association threw a party in Garth's honor and Nashville Mayor Philip Bredesen proclaimed it Garth Brooks Day. Garth turned up fairly disheveled, as though he wasn't expecting the party to be for real. Everyone made speeches. Capitol head Joe Smith said:

What keeps us loving this business and staying in this business is seeing a truly talented artist succeed on this kind of level. It creates an excitement we can all feel. When somebody you hadn't heard of two years ago is sweeping the country and bringing people into record stores because they must have a copy of his music. That's what it's all about. And if you wanted to build a prototype of what a superstar should be, Garth Brooks is it. I have to tell you, it's terrific to be involved with a young man with his character and his kind of solid sense of himself.

Garth was modest as usual:

If I knew this was going to be this big a deal, I would have dressed for it. . . . I've read that Mr. Bowen and Mr. Smith have said that they're not sure how to read me sometimes. Well, I hope this is clear. I want them to be sure and let me know if they're ever leaving and going anywhere, 'cause I want my butt right with you wherever you go. This has been quite a week, and I don't know if this guy deserves it. I just think country music is finally getting what it deserves. It's the number one form of music on this planet.

After the release of *Ropin' the Wind* Garth filled over 23,000 seats in Charlotte, North Carolina, in one hour, seventeen minutes, and that same day sold out shows in Jackson, Mississippi, and Shreveport, Louisiana. In Dallas, Brooks beat Bruce Springsteen's prior speed record by selling all 18,000 seats in thirty-seven minutes. When a second show was added, it sold out in less than an hour.

Billboard's associate director for retail research, Geoff Mayfield, said, "Is he the most popular singer? Gee, I don't know. It's a great story, though. It's obvious that the country audience has grown in the past two or three years, but not to the dimensions that this guy has built his audience."

Clearly Garth was a shoo-in (er, hat-in?) to sweep the Country Music Association's awards in October, but that wasn't a point he felt comfortable addressing. "When people come up and tell you, 'Man, you're gonna take 'em all,' I don't like it. . . . I'd rather have them come up and say, 'You're a low-life bum, and you shouldn't win anything because you're terrible'—and then go out there and take it. That makes me feel good."

He reckons awards don't add up to ability. "It's got nothing to do with how talented you are. There's millions of people [in Nashville] that are ten times more talented than I am. It's just getting your break."

The Country Music Awards took place on October 2 at the Grand Ole Opry. President and Mrs. Bush attended the televised broadcast, and the president found time to make a few remarks about his love of country music: "Country music is a window to the real world. . . . Whenever I want to feel a surge of patriotism or a surge of emotion or a little free advice about Saddam Hussein, I listen to country music." He revealed that on his desk sits a framed quote from the Nitty Gritty Dirt Band: "When you're looking for a rainbow, you can stand a little rain." Fans and artists alike had to go through a metal detector to keep security around the president tight.

Garth won four awards that night and some called it "The Garth Brooks Show." Wearing white tails, black shirt, a white bow tie and white hat, Garth humbly accepted honors for Album, Single, and Video of the Year, as well as Entertainer of the Year. He also sang a passionate rendition of "Shameless."

No one was surprised that Garth's banned

video for "The Thunder Rolls" won as the year's best video. At the podium, director Bud Schaetzle sarcastically thanked TNN: "Domestic violence is something we can stand to learn a little about. I hope that everybody down at TNN knows how much we appreciate their help. We feel like we made our points as filmmakers. People saw it, discussed it, and understood it."

Backstage, Garth, who prides himself on a close relationship with the cable network, leapt forward to do damage control. "The remark made by the producer doesn't stand from Garth Brooks and his corporation. Families fight. You can call me a hypocrite, but I don't think you should air those feelings."

When he won Entertainer of the Year, Garth joked, "This is cool. It's funny how a chubby kid can have fun and they call it entertainment." As usual Garth himself voted for George Strait as entertainer of this and every year. He said, "I love my Georges—George Strait and George Jones." Remembering his audience, Garth sheepishly added, "No offense, Mr. President."

Garth wasn't the only winner. The telecast beat its competitors for ratings. And George Jones said that after the show young people called radio stations and stores asking about this "George Jones fellow Garth Brooks mentioned on TV."

Country Music Week came to an end with the SRO Awards, which pay tribute to the live-performance business. Brooks took top honors as Touring Act of the Year, Joe Harris won Talent Agent of the Year, and Doyle/Lewis won Manager of the Year. Garth was already on the road again, so he didn't attend the banquet.

Inevitably Garth's frequently asked about his ever-increasing stockpile of awards, and he goes to considerable—if bewildering—lengths to keep them in perspective. In 1991 he gave Claudia Perry this classically confused quote:

Awards are tough because they're manipulated by record labels. I guess I'm trying to cover both sides here. They're manipulated for people to win, and they're also manipulated for yourself to win. You can't put much faith at all in awards. They help your career tremendously. The people that truly love you for what you are and what your music is are the ones that show up. The ones who show up because you won an award are the ones that aren't going to be there next year. You have to take them with a grain of salt. . . . It's like a Christmas tree. It brings attention to country music like a Christmas tree does Christmas, but the tree isn't what Christmas is all about.

As for fame itself, Garth admits, "It's a lot

HAT ACTING

Time accused Garth of being more actor than singer, and he's never been secretive about his yen to act. The grapevine reports that Garth's people are reading movie scripts with the singer in mind, but fans might be surprised at the roles that intrigue him.

[Acting] would be way down the road. . . . One role I'd love to do, though, wouldn't have anything to do with cowboys or country. It would be a guy with two personalities, and he was a mass murderer. A bad guy that was just totally flipped out, never knew he was a bad guy. I'd love to do that, sort of like a Jack Nicholson role. . . . Jack Nicholson, even when he's nice, always looks like he's nuts. . . . In the movies you can be anything you want to be and not get in trouble for it. I love to keep people guessing. If I was ever to do movies, I think that's the kind of character I'd like to play—somebody who is just totally nuts.

Garth's not bothered by the *Time* barb:

I would take that as a compliment because that's a statement I've always made. I think a singer has to be a three-minute actor. I think you have to take yourself out of what you have lived and then put it into something that maybe you haven't. For instance, on the song "Alabama Clay". . . there's this farm boy there that left the farm to go to the city and wants to go back to the farm. I was never raised on the farm, but I get to, for three minutes, be this kid and wonder what he's thinking. To me, that's three-minute acting.

easier to cash my checks at the grocery store, but as far as being a star, that's pretty much a four-letter word in my book. I'm just a guy who plays country music and happens to love what he does."

On October 7, the *Nashville Banner* reported that Garth sold 12,000 tickets in just twenty-two minutes for his Murfreesboro concert. Ticket sales were so frenzied that fans jammed Nashville's phone lines—including the government's—between ten and noon!

Some residents felt a compulsion to camp, setting up shop outside the box office four days ahead of the sale date. The fans, mostly college students, listened to tapes, talked, studied, and ate pizzas donated by local radio stations. Even when temperatures dropped to thirty-four degrees one night, they doggedly stayed put. Just as tickets went on sale, one of the campers said, "Nobody got mad at all, nobody had a harsh word, except for these people who showed up this morning and thought they'd bust their way up front. *They* got mad."

Mid-October Garth went to Elkhorn, Nebraska, for the wedding of Stillwater keyboard player David Gant to Susan Polly. Elkhorn's a relatively small community west of Omaha, home to about 1,300 residents. Garth serenaded the hundred wedding guests with "Unchained Melody."

October 15 marked Garth's sitcom debut on an episode of NBC's "Empty Nest." In a bit of typecasting, he played himself. The episode has Barbara (Kristy McNichol) sneaking backstage with Laverne (Park Overall), who faints at the sight of her singing idol. Garth rescues her and becomes friendly with Barbara, a policewoman with ideas about beefing up his backstage security. He offers her a job and she briefly takes to the road as part of his entourage.

Garth sang "The River" and over the closing credits performed a silly, informal version of "Friends in Low Places" before the assembled cast. Kristy McNichol was mesmerized by Garth's talent. "When he sings 'The River' to me, I get chills and I get real emotional—I don't know how to control it. Not that I cry or anything. But you can see the goose bumps and I feel it. It goes through me like a train. His voice is so amazing, but it's more like I'm responding to him as a person, as a soul."

Prior to his appearance Garth admitted he couldn't recall ever seeing Kristy on TV before, though she's been performing all her life and has the Emmys to prove it. He *was* certain he'd seen the work of Richard Mulligan, who used to appear on "Soap," and David Leisure, who played obnoxious Joe Isuzu in commercials.

Both Garth and the folks at NBC had trepidations—working on television's a lot different from making records or touring. The experience left Garth with heightened appreciation for the job of creating a sitcom. "These people work a lot harder than I thought they did. This is tough work. . . . If a song takes six hours to cut, that's a day. Hoo-boy, we worked hard today, we got three minutes on tape. . . . It's a whole lot different here. We gotta be ready for shooting on Tuesday."

During rehearsals Garth realized he had to switch from boss mode to hired-help mode. "I realized, 'Oh, my God. *I am one of the guys.*' So I just said 'yes, sir' and 'no, sir.' It's cool to be one of the boys."

Garth deflected all praise for his acting. "They say, 'You're doing a great job,' and I think, 'Yeah, I can tell why they pay you to act.'" But Garth *did* do a great job because he was playing the character he knows best—himself. The writers of "Empty Nest" must be great Brooks fans; he hardly seems to be acting and his lines sound like outtakes from familiar interviews. Garth's relaxed and natural throughout the episode. His unforced affability shines through, making it a great showcase for his personality. Ever modest, Garth insists, "This show makes me out to be a whole lot bigger star than I am."

Late in October tickets for Garth's November 11 show at the Mississippi Coliseum went on sale, and this time nine fans tried camping out to ensure they'd have seats. Ultimately the determined nine were sent home for security and sanitary reasons, but officials promised them they would get first pick of the tickets.

Why were thirty-five-year-old Peggy Lews and the others camping out in the first place? Well, the Coliseum seats 9,100, but just 56 of those seats are in the front row. . . . Later, fans who didn't balk at paying scalpers' prices were able to secure tickets through newspaper ads, paying from $30 to $150 for the $15 seats.

When Garth finally hit Murfreesboro on November 7, it was his first full-length area concert since 1989. He thrilled the audience with a show *Nashville Banner* critic Jay Orr called, "a stunning display of performance savvy and dynamic charisma never seen by this writer at a country concert and seldom witnessed at rock shows."

Orr dubbed the event a "lovefest" and quoted Brooks shouting, "I love it. I love it. I love it," when fans screamed for more. "This is kind of a first," said Garth. "Not only am I playing in front of what I consider to be my friends, I'm playing in front of my neighbors." In the *Tennessean*, Robert K. Oermann called the show "one of the most striking examples of two-way interplay between performer and crowd I've ever witnessed." Brooks, he said, is "one of the great communicators."

Garth picked up more awards from *Billboard* magazine for Best Male Video and Best Director during a November week when he held the #1, #2, and #5 spots on the country album chart. He played the Summit in Houston midmonth, but that concert was nearly called off. Garth came on-stage before the show to announce that there'd been a bomb threat. The building was swept twice and nothing was found, he said, but anyone who wanted a rain check could get one at the box office. Garth said he hoped they'd stay, because "we're going to blow this place up one way or another tonight!"

In Jackson, Mississippi, fans traded over ten thousand cans of food for the chance to win tickets to Garth's December 6 show. For every ten cans donated for the Community Stewpot, the fan received an envelope. Ten envelopes contained pairs of tickets.

Nineteen ninety-one was also the year Garth first used wireless mikes at the Houston Livestock Show and Rodeo. The new mikes provided freedom of movement that made the act even more spontaneous and zany. "We fell in love with them that night and have used them ever since. We're working on a ski-lift-type rig that will actually take us out over the crowd for this future tour."

Though officially off duty to spend time with Sandy, Garth performed at a benefit for the Sheridan, Wyoming, Theater on December 22. Also on the bill were actor Anthony Zerba and novelist/lyricist Joe Henry, a friend of Garth's from way back. The trio sat on hay bales and read excerpts pertaining to the season from Joe's novel *Lime Creek*. Garth told a local paper, "There ain't no troubles at Christmas. I know people say, 'You're not living in the real world,' but I'm just that way. Christmas is a time for happiness."

Earlier that month in her weekly column for *The Yukon Sun* called "By Brooks' Side," Colleen Brooks wrote that she expected most of her clan home for Christmas. "The good Lord willing, Betsy will be home first, followed by Kelly, followed by Garth and finally Jim and Jerome. Mike won't be able to make it in person but will in Christmas spirit."

The *Sun* also printed a reader's letter that's typical of countless stories credited to this generous performer. It seems Larry Lowe, a truck driver, met Stillwater drummer Mike Palmer and volunteered to hunt down some special equipment during his peregrinations. The next time the band hit Lowe's hometown he delivered the goods (which Palmer paid for).

Lowe's twelve-year-old daughter went along for the delivery—she's a big Brooks fan and wanted autographs. When Mike asked if they were seeing the show, Lowe said no, they hadn't been able to get tickets. Mike offered to locate some freebies.

Palmer was able to find one ticket and said there was a good shot at a second if a concert promoter didn't attend. By the time they got to the concert hall the promoter *had* turned up, but Garth had unearthed another ticket. Lowe's letter ends: "So, beyond belief and twenty minutes before showtime, this premier entertainer . . . is running around a capacity crowd of thousands looking for the promoter to exchange tickets so Mom can sit within sight of her daughter. This is a man that I had only met that afternoon, yet he was doing all this for my loved ones."

Pondering his amazing year, Garth admitted he was baffled. Why was he so hot? What sent country music rocketing to the top of the charts? "I don't think we're going anywhere. I think the crowds are coming over to country," he speculated, adding, "I'm not sure that this is as much a reflection of my music as it is a reflection of the great people that surround me."

Jimmy Bowen said, "He's reflecting the time we live in and reaching the emotions of real people. That's what country music did twenty-five years ago and he's leading us into that again." Perhaps, as Joe Harris claimed, "Country music is now pop music."

Certainly it's being marketed that way—and the change has made a world of difference. Bowen said, "We gave him the priorities of a rock act out of Los Angeles or New York." Manager Pam Lewis is equally pragmatic. She says Garth's sales figures are no accident. "This is a carefully orchestrated plan that's working."

Ultimately Garth's success always comes back to his special relationship with the people who buy his "product." Lewis sees Garth's popularity as "a real testament to the way he treats his fans. He stays after shows to meet the fans and he has always gone the extra mile for them. He still does."

Garth's a bit wary of the adulation. "It kind of scares me. If they feel for me like I feel for some of my heroes—I know myself and I know that I'm not one-tenth of the guy that my heroes are. You'd think that people could find a better hero."

Extraordinary fame carries the seeds of its own destruction. Will people expect so much they'll never be satisfied? Garth wonders if he can top himself. "We used to have the underdog edge, the surprise element, the *ohmigod*-I-didn't-*know*-he-was-gonna-do-*this*-kind-of-thing. But the more you use the shock treatment, the surprise thing, the harder it is to surprise."

"What bothers me is that all success stories have dues to be paid. I haven't paid mine. So I'm wonderin', 'Am I gonna go through holy hell up ahead?'"

By late 1991, Garth had terrific support systems in place. He's surrounded by friends and family. His brother Kelly, an accountant, handles all the tour money management and invests Garth's personal income. Sister Betsy, whom Garth calls "one of the best instrumentalists around," plays bass. Ty England, his guitarist, was a college roommate. Road manager Mick Weber is Garth's best friend from second grade.

Everyone works hard, but Kelly may be clocking more hours since Garth started earning megabucks. While renegotiating his recording deal, Garth said he "had to stop for five minutes so I could go out and breathe because of the ungodly amounts they were talkin' about. My head was spinnin'."

Kelly admits, "Garth threw money around when he had none. Now he's got twenty people on the payroll, 401(k)s, insurance plans, profit sharing. He sees the good that money can do and how fast it goes. He wants to hang on to it." Maybe that's why Garth still drives his old red Silverado pickup—though nowadays it's equipped with a cellular phone!

Garth surprised everyone by announcing he'd take six months off, from December 14 through June, to spend time with Sandy. It would be his first prolonged break from touring since 1989. It would also give him an opportunity to write songs, since he finds it nearly impossible to compose on the road. "This is hopefully going to enable me to write again about real-life situations."

And the hiatus gave Garth time to recharge his batteries before setting out to conquer the world: "To tell you the truth,we're gearing up for our first world tour, which is next year. It's going to be a year and a half of touring. We're going to have to take a big breath and get the stage ready."

A photo op on the set of "Empty Nest."
(photo: Retna)

With the cast of NBC's sitcom "Empty Nest." (photo: Retna)

Backstage at the American Music Awards.
(photo: Ron Galella)

Lofting his American Music Award for the papparazzi. (photo: Retna)

Garth's award from *Billboard*, the music industry's top magazine. (photo: Retna)

Billboard
MUSIC

27th Annual
ACADEMY of
COUNTRY MUSIC
AWARDS

Happiness is a matched pair of awards.

GARTH BROOKS
CRS
CRS

Seems Garth just can't lose!

As the musical guest on "Saturday Night Live" in spring of 1992.

Clutching Sandy and his awards, Garth's the very picture of success.

27TH ANNUAL

(photo: Peyton Hoge)

Chapter Nine
From Strength to Strength

"My career has gotten to where it's like what they say about sex and pizza—when it's great, it's great, and when it ain't great, it's not too bad," joked Garth as 1991 wound down. To judge by his awards and album sales, this is a pizza with everything on it!

By year's end Garth had accumulated more laudatory hardware than the most heavily decorated five-star general. Though he and Sandy share a substantial home in Goodletsville, Tennessee, it seemed inconceivable they would have enough mantel space to accommodate all the trophies. Not necessary, Garth said. "I've got a closet in the guest bedroom, that's where I put them all. I want to get up in the morning and have the score be zero to zero. I really don't want to lose the hunger and the scaredness of possibly losing everything. The most priceless thing I could lose would be the chance to sing. It's a wonderful way to make a living. So I gotta remain hungry. I got the rest of my life after I quit singing to look at those things."

Garth admits he worries the awards are capping a career, not marking its beginning. "A big word for me is seven letters, something George Jones and George Strait have been able to do—*sustain*. I want to be here a long time and not be a flash in the pan."

No doubt he's haunted by other artists who were superhot one year and couldn't get arrested the next. It's happened to Randy Travis and to Kenny Rogers. Maybe that's why Garth persists in saying, "I don't think I'm at the top; I've been fortunate to see the name with no one above [it]—that's cool. I don't think that necessarily means you're at the top. . . . Just because Garth Brooks is going somewhere doesn't mean he's going up. Few people have sustained this level without dying."

At Christmas *Ropin' the Wind* was still ahead of Michael Jackson's *Dangerous* on the *Billboard* charts. Garth rode the top ten for four months and went on to sell another million copies of *Ropin'* after the Country Music Awards show. "It's like a Cheerio. You know, you keep pushing it down, it pops back up," he joked. Of the ninety albums certified platinum in 1991, *Ropin' the Wind* (9 million sold) was the year's top seller.

On January 17, 1992, NBC televised "This Is Garth Brooks," a prime-time, sixty-minute special created by Bud Schaetzle's High Five Production company. Rick Ludwin, senior vice president of specials, variety programs and late night told the papers, "There is rarely a performer who explodes with the popularity that Garth Brooks has. We're tremendously pleased that his first TV special will be with us at NBC."

Two days before the special aired, Garth held a press conference and played his show for reporters. He was typically underdressed, and surprisingly, bearded. He explained he was giving his face a rest after shaving every day for the past two and a half years. He also reminded reporters that he regards himself as two people when he pointed to a poster of himself and called it "this guy back here." He jokingly added, "That explains the weight, because I eat for both of them."

While promoting his special, Garth admitted the sound was cleaned up and much of the concert audio redubbed in the studio. "I fixed a lot. This was my one shot—not so much to represent Garth Brooks but to represent country music the way I thought it was today. As we all know, what comes out live, with the people screaming and all, you just can't hear everybody. You don't always match chord for chord; the vocals are off a lot. I wasn't going to have that represent country music."

Though Garth's a perfectionist, he's worked with Schaetzle enough to trust him with details, so he didn't pester Schaetzle by breathing down his neck. "He'd send me the finished product and I'd call him back and tell him what I felt needed changing, and we'd compromise."

Referring to himself in the third person again, Garth said, "Hopefully this will show [fans] that Garth Brooks is still the same guy. He's just a bum that got lucky and he's still a bum but he's thankful. . . . There's no special guest. It's sort of Garth on Garth, with six or seven songs."

For those who had never seen Garth perform (is that possible?), the special was vintage mayhem. Watching the show, it's readily apparent Garth's not kidding when he claims to have been heavily influenced by stadium rock shows of the 1970s. His extravaganza comes complete with trapdoors, smoke machines, smashing guitars, duck-walking, ramps, Tarzan chest-pounding and rope swinging. Even during the tender ballads Garth's a study in crowd management. He never stops shaking hands, accepting roses and other tokens, pointing at audience members, and pounding his chest.

And in the audience, heavily female but stocked with men in plaid shirts and cowboy hats, everyone's screaming, swaying, crying, singing, and squealing nonstop!

Garth performed some of his best-loved hits including, "If Tomorrow Never Comes," "The Thunder Rolls," and "Friends in Low Places." He wowed the crowd with two Billy Joel songs, "You May Be Right" and "Shameless." Even so, Garth says viewers only saw the tip of the iceberg. "This isn't one hundred percent . . . Time constraints kind of held us to what you see here. It's gotta get wilder, it's gotta get brighter, it's gotta hit you a little harder in the face and in the stomach, too, for me."

Garth revealed how he's able to reach out to those fans sitting miles away in the bleachers. The camera followed Garth on a trek to the top of the stadium, where he said: "Every week before a show, I come out here and I try to sit somewhere the farthest that I can get. And I look down here, and I try to figure out, how am I going to get this person in this seat to somehow feel special?"

"This Is Garth Brooks" is slick. It was filmed with ten cameras shooting as many as forty-four angles per song. The director of photography, Toby Phillips, worked on Madonna's *Truth or Dare*. Schaetzle cleverly contrasts live footage with talking-head segments featuring Betsy, Sandy, Pat Alger, Allen Reynolds, Mark Miller, and Garth.

Betsy calls her little brother "a sincere, big-hearted, knock-kneed, clumsy old cowboy." She says she wishes more men were like him. Garth says, "Taking chances is what got me into this game, and taking chances is probably what will get me thrown out. But one day in the game is worth a year of memories, so I'll make that trade someday if I have to."

The cameras trail Garth climbing among the lights and cables during a rehearsal, terrifying his handlers and generally having a grand old time. "This represents how I live," he explains. "Right beneath me is total solidarity, and to the right and left of me is a straight drop to nowhere."

At the end, Garth concludes, "If what I'm on is the road of life, it's been one hell of a ride." Sure has. He's only the third male solo artist in history to top the 5-million mark with back-to-back albums.

Newsday's Diane Werts commented, "One moment, he's talking about himself aw-shucks and naive like one of those slice-of-life AT&T commercials. The next he's careening around the stage, wild, obsessed, freewheeling. . . . In a way country music hasn't quite seen before, Brooks openly craves the rush that music can provide."

Claudia Perry said, "To this mind, what Brooks manages for an hour is to prove that he's very skilled at figuring out what people want and then giving them just a little bit more. . . . For people who thought country music was sad songs sung by old guys in toupees and sparkly suits, Brooks is a new fool at an old game."

Music Row columnist Jim Bessman wasn't impressed by the TV special. He deemed it manipulative. He said the "rock band antics" seemed contrived and all Garth's "ruminations from the ranch" were ponderous. The "anachronistic cowboy hats and Bic lighters in the audience didn't help."

Garth claimed little interest in his Nielsen ratings, but said he'd be eyeing record sales to see whether the special pulled in new fans. "I'm gonna be watching those album charts two weeks after, and I'm going to see if TV has any kind of a kick in the butt for album charts." As it happened the special won its time slot with a 17.3 rating/28 share. It ranked #19 for the week and gave NBC its highest rated Friday in two years. Roughly 16 million households—or 38 million individuals—tuned in that night.

And Garth must have been delighted when record sales zoomed. At month's end he had sold about 168,000 more copies of *Ropin'* and all told, about 340,000 copies of the three collections. In fact, Garth's were the only albums on the Top 200 to register increased sales that week. *No Fences* went from #10 to #5 and *Garth Brooks* went from #32 to #23. Guess TV kicks butt.

In January, Garth surprised workers at the United Cerebral Palsy telethon when he and Sandy personally stopped by a Nashville TV station to donate $25,000. "They say if you can give what you can afford it isn't really giving. It kind of made us feel good and we just jumped in the truck and got down here 'cause we saw it on TV," he said. Sandy wrote the check.

Just days later, on January 27, en route to the American Music Awards, Sandy collapsed at the Los Angeles airport. Three months pregnant with Taylor Mayne and utterly exhausted, she came dangerously near a miscarriage. During the flight from Nashville Sandy began feeling ill. By the time they landed, around two P.M., she collapsed. Garth was scheduled to perform at the American Music Awards that night, but canceled his appearance to stick by Sandy's side and announced he would not attend any awards shows—including the Grammys—unless Sandy could be there.

POLITICS II: GARTH JUST SAYS NO. . . TO VOTING

During an interview published near Valentine's Day in the election year of 1992, Garth told a *USA Weekend* reporter, "I've never voted. Politics used to be what's right or wrong. Now it's just what's Democrat or Republican. There's never been a man who's run for president who I thought would make a difference."

(That's ironic, since he once told Britain's *Country Music People*, "I am a common man with a common vote. I'm just a patriotic citizen.")

Garth's comment provoked some media backlash around Nashville. In the *Banner*, M. Lee Smith, publisher of the *Tennessee Journal*, admonished Brooks, "For Garth to suggest the person who occupies the Oval Office doesn't make a difference would be almost laughable if it didn't reflect such a serious misunderstanding of our government. . . . Maybe Garth just didn't want to alienate any of his fans. After all, George Bush is a conspicuous fan of country music, and . . . Bill Clinton appeals to the pickup-and-beer crowd who are also Garth Brooks fans."

How can you hope to be a good role model for kids, asked Smith, if you don't vote?

Music critic Robert K. Oermann asked the same question in the *Tennessean*. The people who vote least frequently, he noted, are "the young, the poor, the black, the disenfranchised, the people whose lives inspire country songs. Those are your people, Garth. They think, like you do, that they can't make a difference. . . . They think this isn't their government. And they're right because they haven't claimed it."

Vote, urged Oermann. Vote because "you should set an example for the average Americans who love you. If you think one person can't make a difference, just look at your own career and its impact on popular culture."

Does he or doesn't he? Only Garth's election board knows for sure. . . .

At the hospital doctors told Sandy she and the baby were okay, but cautioned her against flying for the remainder of her pregnancy. She and Garth traveled home by bus along with Sandy's mom, who flew to L.A. to be with the frightened couple.

Even in absentia, Garth won awards for Favorite Country Artist, Country Single, and Country Album that night.

In February, Capitol Nashville changed its name to Liberty Records, and Jimmy Bowen was heard boasting that most of the United States' music would emanate from Nashville by the turn of the century.

Garth won a Grammy that month for Best Country Male Vocal but, as promised, didn't attend the ceremonies. He was interviewed for *TV Guide* and gave classic answers now familiar to his fans. Awards don't mean much but he's sure glad to get them. Country music hasn't crossed into pop, pop's come to country. On that subject Garth added, "I'm proud to say I belong to country music and will stay there until they kick me out." He expressed delighted surprise at the video channel VH-1's terrific response to his videos, and as for TNN, well, he hinted they'd benefit from some competition. The Nashville Chamber of Commerce put Garth's photo on the cover of their vacation guide. Butch Spyridon, convention and visitors bureau chief, justified this, saying, "Garth Brooks is the hottest thing in country music, and we are Music City, so it makes sense to put Garth out front."

Throughout the winter Garth toiled to learn to play Elton John's "Candle in the Wind" on the piano because he wanted to include it in his 1992 tour. He also supervised renovations to his Goodletsville mansion. Rumor has it he's creating a virtual Garth Brooks Recreation Center! He allegedly told a source the addition will have an indoor softball field, horse ring, gym, and more, so when it rains he never has to go outside.

By March, Sandy was well enough to accompany Garth to the Country Radio Seminar held in Nashville's Acuff Theater. Garth starred in the Superfaces show, playing a sixty-minute set for the conventioneers. He ran through old favorites and showcased some new tunes from the September release.

Before Garth could perform an encore, the Academy of Country Music made a Special Achievement Award presentation. Garth said, "Sometimes a person stays the same but the world changes around them, and sometimes the person changes but the world stays the same. I hope in your eyes I haven't changed." Garth also called Sandy to the stage and crowed over his still svelte wife, turning her sideways to display her "bump." "For people who have been asking," he announced, "they let her out tonight. . . . The good Lord's been with us."

They also announced that the baby was a girl. In her *Yukon Sun* column, Colleen expressed amusement that for *once* she, had learned about something in Garth's life from the horse's mouth instead of reading it in the tabloids!

Garth and Sandy really had to announce Taylor's sex because fans were bombarding them with gifts and it seemed sensible to direct them a little. Their brand-new nursery is done up in Disney characters. "Sandy is a Mickey Mouse freak. She likes the Disney characters, Goofy, all of them." On March 20, Beth Stein, a reporter for the *Nashville Banner,* told readers she had had lunch with Sandy during the ASCAP dedication ceremonies and discovered the good folks at Disney were sending the Brookses plenty of trimmings for the nursery.

Garth said he offered his dad a million dollars to raise their little one because "I'm not sure I can do half the job my parents did." Troyal turned him down, saying, "No, my job is to spoil it and give it back."

At the March festivities "christening" ASCAP's new headquarters, president Morton Gould gave Garth the newly created Voice of Music Award "for having made a singular breakthrough in the field of music that has generated widespread excitement within the music industry and among the general public." "Cool," said Garth.

He added, "Let me warn you, with the talent that's in country music today, and in all the other forms of music, I have a feeling ASCAP will be giving this out a lot more." Garth thanked God and Bob Doyle, and bluntly said, "You must always take care of what feeds you. To the people of ASCAP I just say, please take care of the people who feed you, and that is the writers. They're wonderful people. They often sit in the shadows so many times."

In March Garth appeared on "Saturday Night Live," hosted by John Goodman. Garth also visited Eddie Murphy to sing on Murphy's "Yeah Song," an exuberant up-tempo number featuring vocals by a host of recognizable names including Hammer, Stevie Wonder, Jon Bon Jovi and Michael Jackson. The only lyric is "Yeah."

According to the account in *Life*, Eddie greeted Garth by saying, "You're a little baby face, man." After he played Brooks the track with all its famous voices, Garth said, "I'm not a major talent. I'm a product of the people. I don't know if I can do something like this, but I'd sure like to try." Murphy replied, "Well . . . I've heard you sing, so I know you can sing on key." Then Garth let it rip and Murphy squealed with delight.

March was also when residents of Yukon debated the merits of naming a street after Garth—and it was quite a tussle. The town council held a public hearing to see whether Eleventh Street should be renamed Garth Brooks Boulevard. The *Sun*'s editorial page came out in favor of the change. "Mr. Brooks deserves all the accolades we can give him. After all, he's a hometown boy . . . an entertainer that the whole world is watching." And, they continued, the debate alone was generating so much publicity that perhaps Yukon's economy would be improved by an influx of tourists.

Nay voters pointed out the trouble and expense for residents who had to change their address, Garth's youth and relative lack of achievement, plus the fact that he not only lives in Nashville, but spent close to a million dollars to buy his folks a sprawling 151-acre ranch north of the Yukon city limits.

Ultimately the ayes had it, Garth Brooks Boulevard became official on May 31, with Garth on hand for the dedications. Town elders were worried about disappearing street signs, so they hung all but one on streetlights. City manager Stan Griel explained, "You need a hook and ladder truck to get one down from the streetlight." Souvenier replicas of the sign sell for $20, while three sizes of replicas of Yukon's water tower can be had for $10–$20. All profits will benefit the Yukon Museum Association and Chamber of Commerce.

In April, Garth was driving into Nashville from his house and saw a woman standing by her truck, which had broken down. True to form, he stopped, collected her, and arranged to have the truck towed to his garage. He also arranged to have all bills for towing and repairs sent to *him*. The woman was so grateful she returned to the garage to find out where she could deliver two apple pies she had baked by way of a thank-you. What a good neighbor!

In April, Garth and Sandy—looking radiant and healthy—appeared at the Academy of Country Music awards show. They sat dead center in the front row, alongside Reba McEntire. Garth sang "The River" and collected awards for Male Vocalist of the Year and Entertainer of the Year. At the podium, Garth sent best wishes to fellow singer Doug Stone, who had had a quadruple bypass that afternoon. He also thanked all the fans and colleagues who'd been asking after Sandy's health. She proudly rubbed her growing belly, grinning from ear to ear.

Backstage, however, Garth admitted his life's been in turmoil. "I'm upside down and I have this thing in my heart telling me the responsibilities of being a father.' He talked seriously of retirement. "For the last few years, business always came before family. But the future will be extremely different. If that upsets people, I'm sorry. But with a kid coming, your life has to be slower. Years are one thing you can't buy back."

Despite the happy ending to Sandy's health scare and all his awards, Brooks claimed the previous six months had been "pure hell. What could go wrong, did go wrong." He also talked about his debt to Burt Reynolds, who offered Garth support in the form of a cautionary letter. Reynolds, it seems, wrote to tell Brooks "how rarefied the air is on top. He also wrote how painful the drop can be."

Falling out of favor is one of Garth's biggest fears. "It's great being on top, but you always

GARTH'S VIDEOS

Though country music's resurgent popularity is partly due to increased media exposure—i.e., television—Garth has managed a slew of hit singles without making many videos. Fact of it is, Garth doesn't like them. "I'm not a fan of videos, and if the video can't take a song into a new dimension, I don't want to do it."

Garth's so serious about this that he withheld a video shot for "Friends in Low Places" because the finished product didn't meet his requirements. "The video circled it in and narrowed it down, so I said, 'No, let's don't even show that.'"

At this writing Garth has released just three videos. "If a video can bring another dimension or a new look to the song or make it more acceptable, I'm fine for it. The video for 'The Dance' took the song and made it something else. I think it meant more to people than just a good love gone bad."

For "The Dance," Garth used footage of slain historic figures and other sorely missed individuals, such as John Wayne, JFK, Martin Luther King, Jr., singer Keith Whitley, rodeo rider Lane Frost, and the *Challenger* astronauts, to take the song beyond its apparent meaning, making it a metaphor for life, not just romantic love. You don't have to relate to all of these people, says Garth. If you relate to even one of them, that's great.

The clips work well because they're not overly familiar, so they escape being trite. Garth and his team selected stirring images of King and Kennedy with their families, and one of John Wayne stooping to kiss his wife as they leave a plane. Film of Keith Whitley shows him slow-dancing with his wife, singer Lorrie Morgan.

According to *Country Music* magazine (Jan/Feb 1991), "it is reliably reported in Nashville that [Garth] caused one of his music videos to be reedited at least six times, overriding budgetary considerations and the fact that everybody else in his camp was satisfied with the first effort, because of his demanding perfectionism." In interviews Garth talks about the fuss he caused over "The Dance," so it's a safe guess this is the video in question.

Tony Arata, who wrote "The Dance," admits his song didn't start out having anything to do with JFK or King, but he loves the video. Arata was "bowled over" the first time he saw it. "I was just overwhelmed and said, 'Thank you.' I don't think I would've ever come up with that."

Garth says, "If I should leave this world unexpectedly, I hope they play 'The Dance' for me." In other words, he says, "Don't cry for me, because I had the time of my life!"

The first video Garth ever made was for "If Tomorrow Never Comes." Garth opened up the song to include the special relationship between parents and children. Though it was done quickly on a small budget, the video's a charming testament to family love. The little girl acting as Garth and Sandy's child is Aubrey Gatlin, daughter of Steve Gatlin, one of the Gatlin Brothers.

The video meshes footage of Garth alone in a Victorian parlor, strumming and singing, with footage of Aubrey romping outdoors, cuddling with her grandmother and playing with Sandy and Garth.

There's an interesting postscript to this video, Garth reveals on the compilation tape. When he and Sandy first moved to Nashville, they used to drive around admiring houses, fantasizing about which one they'd like to live in someday. Their favorite was a gorgeous Victorian that was sold through a mail order catalog and assembled at its current location in the 1920s. Imagine Garth and Sandy's surprise when the video's producer came to show them photos of a great location he'd found—and it was the same house! That's karma for you.

By far the most talked about video in Garth's collection is the clip for "The Thunder Rolls." Garth worked with director Bud Schaetzle and technicians from "Twin Peaks" on this story of domestic violence and adultery. In the video he's a womanizing husband with a violent streak who turns on his family once too often. He's blasted into eternity by his pistol-wielding, battered wife. The video took three and a half days to shoot and Garth endured four hours of makeup each day to become its bearded, brown-eyed villain.

Long before he cut it for the album, Garth played the song live, complete with its third verse, which clearly describes the murder. When it came time to record the tune on *No Fences*, producer Allen Reynolds said the verse made him uncomfortable. Garth left it out. Some time passed. Eventually he resumed playing the entire song in concert. Audiences loved it, and Garth decided to use the video to link the record to the original song. Though the third verse isn't sung for the video, the action spells it out.

When Garth saw the finished video, he gasped. "With 'The Dance' I meant to make a statement, but with this one I just meant to make a video to a song. When it was over, it was like, 'Oh, my God, what have I done?' When people ask what I'm trying to say with this video, I'm already prepared to tell them, 'I don't think it's what I'm trying to say. I think it's what people are seeing.'"

Initially the country music TV stations were supportive. Ric Trask, the manager of programming at Country Music Television (CMT), said, "I think we're going to get a lot of response. I don't know which way it will go. I'm impressed that Garth has gone out on a limb. I'm really knocked over by the production. It's tremendously innovative." The video aired in heavy rotation as pick of the week for seven days, then CMT dropped it, allegedly because viewers objected.

Yes, viewers may have found the enactment of domestic violence distasteful (though *People* said, "Farrah Fawcett's . . . 'The Burning Bed' makes the video look like a 'Honeymooners' episode"), but CMT is owned by Opryland USA and Group W Satellite Communications. Opryland also owns The Nashville Network (TNN), which banned the video without ever showing it. It's fairly likely that CMT felt pressure to follow suit. The PBS show "New Country Video" also refused to air the video, claiming, "It's well done, but it's too graphic for our audience."

TNN's program director, Paul Corbin, said, "The violence is so strong and so graphic that it leaves you with a helpless feeling. We felt that it could air if it was put in the proper context." TNN said they'd play the clip if Brooks added a disclaimer at the end giving an 800 number where viewers could get information and/or help. They felt the "depiction of domestic violence is excessive and without an acceptable resolution."

A disclaimer is fine, said Garth, but I won't film it myself, since that would look like an apology. "I would have never, ever, done something TNN and CMT couldn't use, but I'm not going to change what I do to fit their standards."

Bud Schaetzle commented that Garth is "a real principled guy and the video is a labor of love . . . a real heartfelt attempt to create a debate about the topic. . . . Garth is a state-of-the-art artist, and I don't see any reason why he shouldn't be making state-of-the-art videos."

TNN wouldn't produce their own disclaimer. Why? Officially, they said, "A message from anyone other than Brooks, who is held in high esteem by our viewers who would view the music video, would be less than effective in resolving the violent scenario created by the video."

At this time, Bob Baker, CMT's director of operations, said, "I'm yanking the thing. We are a music channel. We are an entertainment medium. We are not news. We are not social issues. We are not about domestic violence, adultery, and murder. We go into thirteen million living rooms. We went out on a limb and took a shot. Now we have made an equally conscious decision with the input of our viewers to pull it." According to Baker, viewer response started out evenly divided but quickly grew negative.

Garth countered, "I'm kind of disappointed . . . they want to see the good side of real life but they want to turn their backs to the bad side." He carefully walked the line, proving himself an expert politician. Garth managed to express his frustrations without openly antagonizing the cable networks.

He told the *Nashville Banner*, "TNN has standards. Garth Brooks has standards. For some crazy reason, on this occasion the two did not cross. I know now where I stand with TNN. If my video runs on there, I should be proud because I have a video that's family entertainment and fits their standards. And if I don't, they're not going to bend and wave just so I can have it run. I want my video to show because of what it is, not who it is."

Garth's stature over at TNN wobbled but didn't topple. In the thick of the debate, Paul Corbin complimented him. "It's not a situation where we have good guys versus bad guys. It's just a philosophical difference. [Garth's] behavior in all of this has been sterling."

Garth said, "I didn't want the thing like Madonna, where it says, 'Banned by TNN, you've got to see this thing.'" Of course that's precisely what happened! One Nashville radio station, WSIX-FM, showed the video several times at the Wrangler in Murfreesboro during a live remote, and local television shows picked up the video, using it to back up discussions about domestic violence.

On May 8, 1991, Tower records on West End Avenue in Nashville announced they'd show the video hourly from four to eight p.m. daily. Store manager Michael Tannen explained, "We want to give people the chance to come in and see the video and judge for themselves about whether it should be shown. If they're not going to see the video on TNN or CMT, where are they going to be able to see it?"

VH-1, which primarily airs pop videos, jumped on the Brooks bandwagon and included his video in their limited country lineup.

Mostly, the publicity worked in Garth's favor and sales flourished. Yet Garth's not obsessed by the bottom line, and good sales didn't quell his unhappiness: "It crushed me. I was shocked. I was so hurt. To go out there and do the makeup every morning for four hours—instead of just throwing some paint up on a sheet and dancing around—and then to get cut off by someone in the middle was just a big crock. As far as music videos, I don't have any desire to do another one. I'd like to stay out of it for three or four years."

How shocked could he have been, really? In April of 1991, Garth told a reporter for the *Nashville Banner*, "Believe me, man, this one takes it far out of what the words say."

After the ban, Garth made the following comments:

> *Unfortunately, violence for me has always been a way of life. It's something very real where I come from. I think Oklahoma City, the world in homicides per year when I was growing up; they would average one or two a day. You'd turn on the news, and someone had been killed. It was no big thing. Violence was a way of life the same way love and happiness was. Death, after all, is as much a part of living as being born.*
>
> *Real life has brought me here. This video is a side of real life people . . . don't really want to see. I refuse to do a video that is just ordinary. It wastes the viewers' time and mine and my label's money. . . . It doesn't bother me that TNN and CMT have decided not to run the video. I'm not angry at them. It's just that I've worked this hard on something that's not getting a chance to be seen. My only hope is this hasn't destroyed our chance to get other videos aired on TNN, and they've assured me it hasn't.*
>
> *The video has already done in two days what I hoped it would do in a lifetime . . . making people aware of a situation which unfortunately exists in our society and causing them to discuss it, sometimes even heatedly. That's what I want my music to do, and I simply refuse to make a no-brainer video and will not do so in the future.*

It's puzzling that neither station compromised by creating their own disclaimers or airing the video late at night when children wouldn't be watching. David M. Ross, editor of *Music Row*, denounced this incident as one more instance of Nashville shooting itself in the foot. "As an industry we continually grapple against the bias of the L.A./New York media gatekeepers who . . . view our industry as if 'Hee Haw' was a documentary."

Throughout May, Garth's video was the subject of editorials and made news. In the *Tennessean*, writer Thomas Goldsmith expressed concern that a lack of rivalry between the nation's top country networks (engendered by their blood ties) "denies country fans the chance to see something that could entertain, enlighten or even change their lives." An editorial in the *Tennessean* took a similar stance. It applauded Garth for taking a risk and came out in favor of the people's—not corporate—choice.

Music Row's Bob Paxman and Jim Bessman debated the ban in print. Bessman argued: "To devise a scenario legitimating spousal murder—which doesn't happen in the song [sic]—is to me the real crime here. As for Garth, he's an unconvincing wife-beater." Paxman countered that the video doesn't advocate violence, it abhors it. He concluded, "The story line shocks, it scars and scares; real life happens that way."

Garth is right—his video generated a public debate about domestic violence and made him a kind of hero to battered women, who too frequently feel they have no voice. Many victims and victims' advocates openly praised Garth. Shelters throughout the country showed the video to spark discussion in group counseling, and several radio stations nationwide sponsored listener viewing nights, donating ticket receipts to shelters and abuse programs.

Susan Canon, director of Nashville's Project to End Abuse Through Counseling and Education, praised the video. "I think that it portrays very realistically a serious problem in America. Every fifteen seconds a woman in this country is battered. Six million are battered every year, and four thousand of them die every year."

She spoke out against the ban: "The men said, 'This is banned because this is what really goes on and people don't want to know what's going on."

have to realize that you can go down that ladder of success just as quickly. Some people have told me the drop can be even quicker than the climb. It's the fans who determine your fate in this business."

Those people were the Gatlin Brothers, who cornered Garth backstage at the Grand Ole Opry. Garth told *Life* reporter Charles Hirshberg about his conversation with the members of this popular singing group:

They proceeded to tell me, for three hours, how not to screw up. "Remember . . . the candle burns out. Curves go up, and then they go down. Take care of your relationship with your wife. Don't do the drug thing. If anybody says the words 'tax shelter' to you, run like hell. Invest in safe things. Try to get in a position where you can walk away from the music business, should that become necessary. Above all: Never, ever play music because you have to. Music should be love, fun, joy. Music will take care of the money if you let the music take care of itself."

Yet for all this good advice, Garth admits the pressure closed in on him like an iron fist. He was juggling commitments to television, endorsements, and other ventures that included freezing a million dollars in collateral so his band could finance morgages. Garth felt stretched and ready to snap, trapped in a lifesyle for all the wrong reasons.

After carefully listing the issues troubling him, Garth began changing. He canceled some agreements and retreated as much as possible. He also approached contract negotiations with Liberty Records like a warrior preparing for battle." The fact is, I'm just tired. I'm beat up. . . . I feel I've earned my wings, and I'm just not as happy as I ought to be. Now I'm bringing a lot to the table, and I feel I'm due a lot in return."

On June 2, Garth began his six-month, seventy-eight-date tour, scheduled to visit forty-one cities and wind up on December 12 in Detroit. He played the first show in Denver, where fans pelted the stage with baby gifts. Tickets for this tour are a standard $17 everywhere in the country, but they're nearly impossible to get. He sold 25,000 tickets for Tacoma, Washington, in under an hour. Officials at the Texas state fair said they expected 10,000-12,000 fans to turn out for Garth, and 55,000 wanted tickets! Fans in Idaho and Montana turned the box office into "Camp Garth" when they lined up long before tickets went on sale. Garth played just two dates in his home state—Oklahoma City on August 21, and Tulsa on the twenty-second.

Come 1993, Garth and Stillwater will be swinging through Europe and Australia. Garth's excited about heading overseas, where he's had limited exposure so far. He played London's Cambridge Theater in 1991, but the audience was mostly American servicemen. Garth realizes touring abroad will be like starting over: "It's gonna be hard because I've got accustomed to being spoiled. It's gonna be difficult to get back into people who don't know who you are. . . . You know, the U.S. is a huge place but it's really not that big, especially when you start taking gulps of fifteen thousand people at a show. . . . So I said, let's hit the world, to where when we come back to the States, it's something special."

Jimmy Bowen isn't worried about Garth's success at home or overseas. He's justifiably proud of Liberty's top star: "Garth Brooks has set a new benchmark, and you're going to see him continue to succeed because he's got his head on straight and he's got some very creative ideas on how to reach people. He's showing you how you act when you earn this kind of success. He's a fine young man."

What else does the future hold for Garth Brooks? He's not one to slow down, that's for sure. On his special, Garth said, "You can always smell the roses when you're running with them in your hand."

Fans should keep their ears peeled for a duet between Garth and his mom, called "Picking Up After You," written by Brooks and Kent Blazy. "When we do it, Mom and I will record it," says Garth. "If it's never on an album, it don't matter. It's just something for me and my mother."

Meanwhile, Garth will undoubtedly continue to grow as a performer and a human being as he fights to exorcise the ghosts that continue to haunt him: "Life is a war between wrong and right, and you're merely a person who has become a soldier. . . . Just because the good Lord gives you a gift doesn't mean that it's necessarily going to be used for good. I've used my gift for evil before, and I regret it seriously. I've used it for physical relationships. I've used it to get what I wanted and then found out what I wanted was so very wrong."

When the clouds blow away—and luckily they do—Garth views his future optimistically: "I'm the entertainer I've always wanted to be and the husband I never thought I could be. I'd never mean this egotistically, but I'm very happy with who I am right now, which is a big change for me."

Two weeks ahead of her July 21 due date, Taylor Mayne Pearl arrived, weighing in at a healthy seven pounds, four ounces. Garth was on hand to help Sandy through the delivery, performed by Dr. Leslie Breiten. Garth told reporters, "I even got to cut her umbilical cord and just about cut the nurse's finger off I was so dang nervous and happy. . . . [I] couldn't see because I was bawling my eyes out the whole time. I was trying not to, but I couldn't help it."

According to Garth the delivery was swift and uncomplicated. "I had heard these were long processes. As the day went on, we were laughing and joking as she went through her contractions. The next thing I know, the doctors were in there. . . . After an hour, it was there." Asked to describe Taylor, Garth said, "She's perfect. And Sandy is perfect. . . . I'm shocked that both of them are doing this well. Everything is just wonderful."

(photo: Peyton Hoge)

"Product"

Each year brings a new Garth Brooks album—or what the folks at Liberty (Garth included) call "product." Die-hard fans can also find Garth warbling such Christmas carols as "Silent Night" and "God Rest Ye Merry, Gentlemen" on seasonal compilations featuring a host of country performers. Garth also sings alongside Trisha Yearwood on her hit "Like We Never Had a Broken Heart."
Garth's albums are:

Garth Brooks. 1989, Capitol Nashville. Produced by Allen Reynolds. Recorded and mixed by Mark Miller at Jack's Tracks Recording Studio, Nashville. Mastered by Denny Purcell at Georgetown Masters.

Musicians: drums—Milton Sledge; bass—Mike Chapman; electric guitars—Christ Leuzinger; acoustic guitars—Mark Casstevens; keyboards—Bobby Wood; steel guitar—Bruce Bouton; fiddle—Rob Hajacos; strings—The Nashville String Machine (Carl Gorodetzky, Dennis Molchan, Pamela Sixfin, John Borg, George Binkley III, Roy Christensen, Gary Vanosdale); string arrangements—Charles Cochran.

"This album is dedicated to the loving memories of Jim Kelley and Heidi Miller."

1. "Not Counting You" by Garth Brooks
2 "I've Got a Good Thing Going" by Bastian, Mahl, Brooks
3 "If Tomorrow Never Comes" by K. Blazy, G. Brooks
4. "Everytime That it Rains" by Stefl, England Brooks
5. "Alabama Clay" by L. Cordle, R. Scaife
6. "Much Too Young (To Feel This Damn Old)" by R. Taylor, G. Brooks
7. "Cowboy Bill" by L. Bastian, E. Berghoff
8. "Nobody Gets Off in This Town" by L. Bastian, D . Blackwell
9. "I Know One" by Jack Clement
10. "The Dance" by Tony Arata

No Fences. 1990, Capitol Nashville. Produced by Allen Reynolds. Recorded and mixed by Mark Miller at Jack's Tracks Recording Studio, Nashville. Mastered by Denny Purcell at Georgetown Masters
Musicians: acoustic guitars—Pat Alger, Johnny Christopher, Mark Casstevens, Chris Leuzinger; bass—Mike Chapman, Milton Sledge; drums—Milton Sledge; electric guitar—Chris Leuzinger; electric piano, piano, and keyboards—Bobby Wood; steel guitar—Bruce Bouton; upright string bass—Edgar Meyer; fiddle—Rob Hajacos; strings—Nashville String Machine (George Binkley III, John Borg, Carl Gorodetzky, Lee Larrison, Dennis Molchan, Pamela Sixfin, Mark Tanner, Garry Vanosdale, Kristin Wilkinson); string arrangements—Charles Cochran.
Band and crew of Stillwater: Tim Bowers—bass guitar, vocals; Dave Gant—keyboards, fiddles, vocals; James Garver—guitars, fiddles, vocals; Steve McClure—steel and electric guitars; Ty England—acoustic guitars, vocals; Mike Palmer—drums, percussion; Dan Hines—sound; Brian Petree—stage manager; Al"Shaggy" Barclay—bus driver; Kelly Brooks—money man.

"This album is dedicated to all who hear the music and have the courage to dance."

1. "The Thunder Rolls" by Pat Alger, Garth Brooks
2. "New Way to Fly" by Kim Williams, Garth Brooks
3. "Two of a Kind, Workin' on a Full House" by Bobby Boyd, Warren Dale Haynes, Dennis Robbins
4. "Victim of the Game" by Mark D. Sanders, Garth Brooks
5. "Friends in Low Places" by Dewayne Blackwell, Bud Lee
6. "Wild Horses" by Bill Shore, David Wills
7. "Unanswered Prayers" by Pat Alger, Larry B. Bastain, Garth Brooks
8. "Same Old Story"by Tony Arata
9. "Mr. Blue" by Dewayne Blackwell
10. "Wolves" by Stephanie Davis

Ropin' the Wind. 1991, Capitol Nashville. Produced by Allen Reynolds. Recorded analog and digitally mixed at Jack's Tracks Recording Studio, Nashville by Mark Miller. Mastered by Denny Purcell at Georgetown Masters.

Musicians: bass—Mike Chapman; drums, percussion—Milton Sledge; percussion—Kenny Malone; keyboards—Bobby Wood; electric guitars—Chris Leuzinger; acoustic guitars—Mark Casstevens; fiddle—Rob Hajacos; steel guitar, lap steel, Dobro—Bruce Bouton; mandolin—Sam Bush; Dobro—Jerry

Douglas; acoustic bass—Edgar Meyer; strings—The Nashville String Machine (George Binkley III, Roy Christensen, Conni Ellisor, Carl Gorodetzky, Richard Grosjean, Anthony LaMarchina, Lee Larrison, Theodore Madsen, Dennis Molchan, Pamela Sixfin, Gary Vanosdale, Kristin Wilkinson); string arrangements—Charles Cochran.
Band and crew of Stillwater: Dave Gant—keyboards, fiddle, vocals; Brent Dannen—stage sound; Steve McClure—steel, electric guitars; Gaylon Moore—bus driver; Crom Tidwell—merchandise; Kelly Brooks—money man; Mike Palmer—drums, percussion; Jim Payne—bus driver; Brian Petree—stage manager; Bradley Martin—merchandise; Ty England—acoustic guitars, vocals; Steve Southerland—bus driver; Mick Weber—road manager; Dave Butzler—lighting director; Betsy Smittle—bass guitar, vocals; Mark Greenwood—stage manager; Dan Heins—house sound; James Garver—electric guitars, percussion, vocals; John McBride—production manager.

"This album is dedicated to Reba's 'Crazy Eight,' to their families and friends. I wish God's strength and understanding upon you."

1. "Against the Grain" by Bruce Bouton, Larry Corle, Carl Jackson
2. "Rodeo" by Larry Bastian
3. "What She's Doing Now" by Pat Alger, Garth Brooks
4. "Burning Bridges" by Stephanie C. Brown, Garth Brooks
5. "Papa Loved Mama" by Kim Williams, Garth Brooks
6. "Shameless" by Billy Joel
7. "Cold Shoulder" by Kent Blazy, Kim Williams, Garth Brooks
8. "We Bury the Hatchet" by Wade Kimes, Garth Brooks
9. "In Lonesome Dove" by Cynthia Limbaugh, Garth Brooks
10. "The River" by Victoria Shaw, Garth Brooks

Video Compilation

Garth Brooks (Includes "The Dance," "If Tomorrow Never Comes," and "The Thunder Rolls," plus interview footage of Garth discussing how and why each video was made, and live-performance footage.)
1991 Capitol Nashville Home Video
Approximate running time: thirty minutes
All songs produced by Allen Reynolds
Compilation video coordinator: Sherri Halford
Compilation video director: Bud Schaetzle
Compilation video producer: Martin Fischer
Editor: Mike McNamara

"The Dance." Director: John Lloyd Miller. Producer: Marc Ball

"If Tomorrow Never Comes." Director: John Lloyd Miller. Executive producer: Cynthia Biedermann. Producer: Kitty Moon

"The Thunder Rolls." Director: Bud Schaetzle. Producer: Martin Fischer

Garth's adamant about quality control, so all his T-shirts are thick, heavy cotton.

"Product," circa summer 1992.

garth brooks

Garth says music is his soapbox. Clearly T-shirts are also billboards.

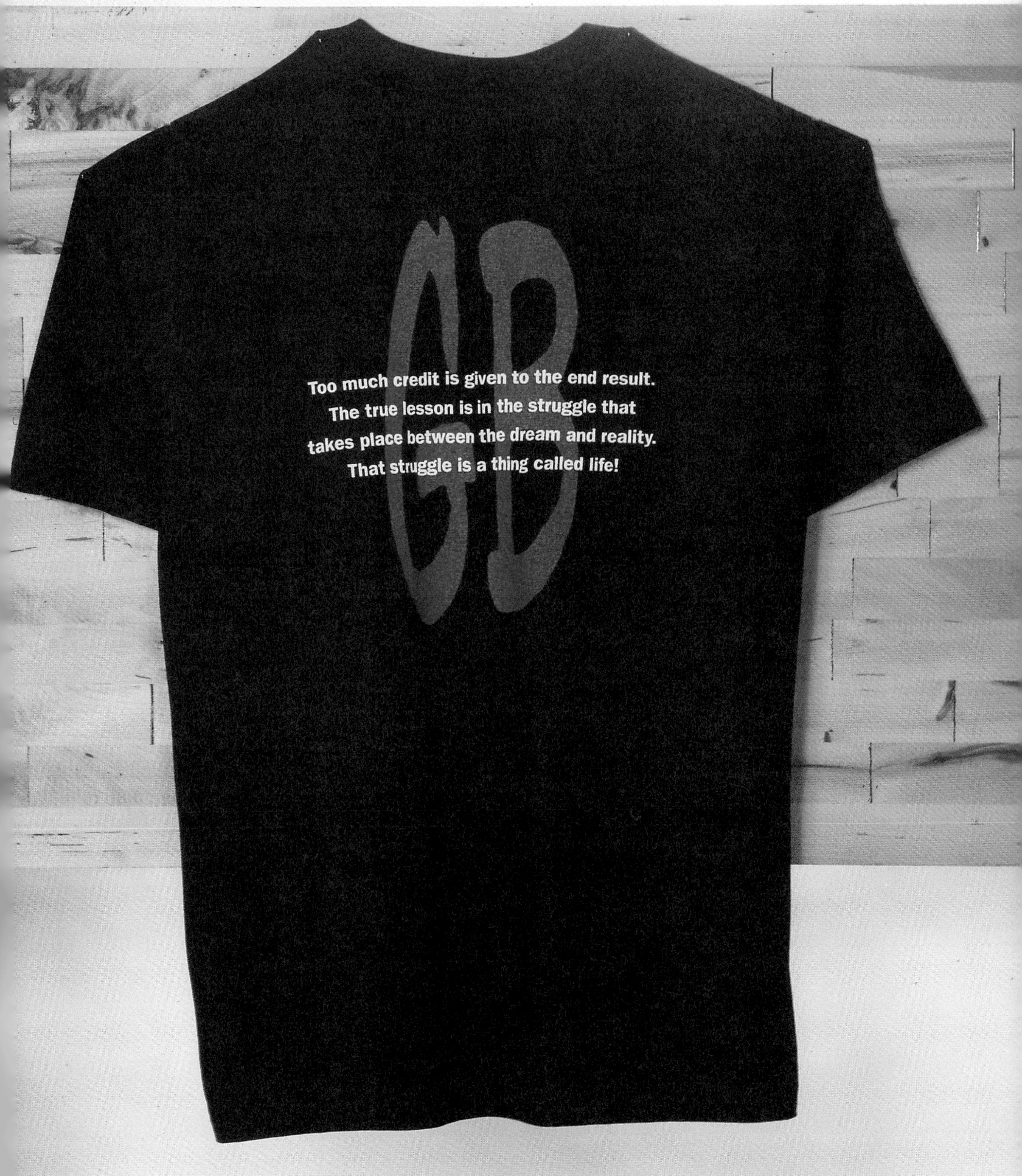

GB

Too much credit is given to the end result.
The true lesson is in the struggle that
takes place between the dream and reality.
That struggle is a thing called life!

T-shirt sales at concerts probably generate more revenue for Garth's Blue Rose corporation than the tickets themselves.

ropin'
the wind

Honesty is Garth's trademark, so "believable" has become his buzzword.

BROOKS
BELIEVABLE

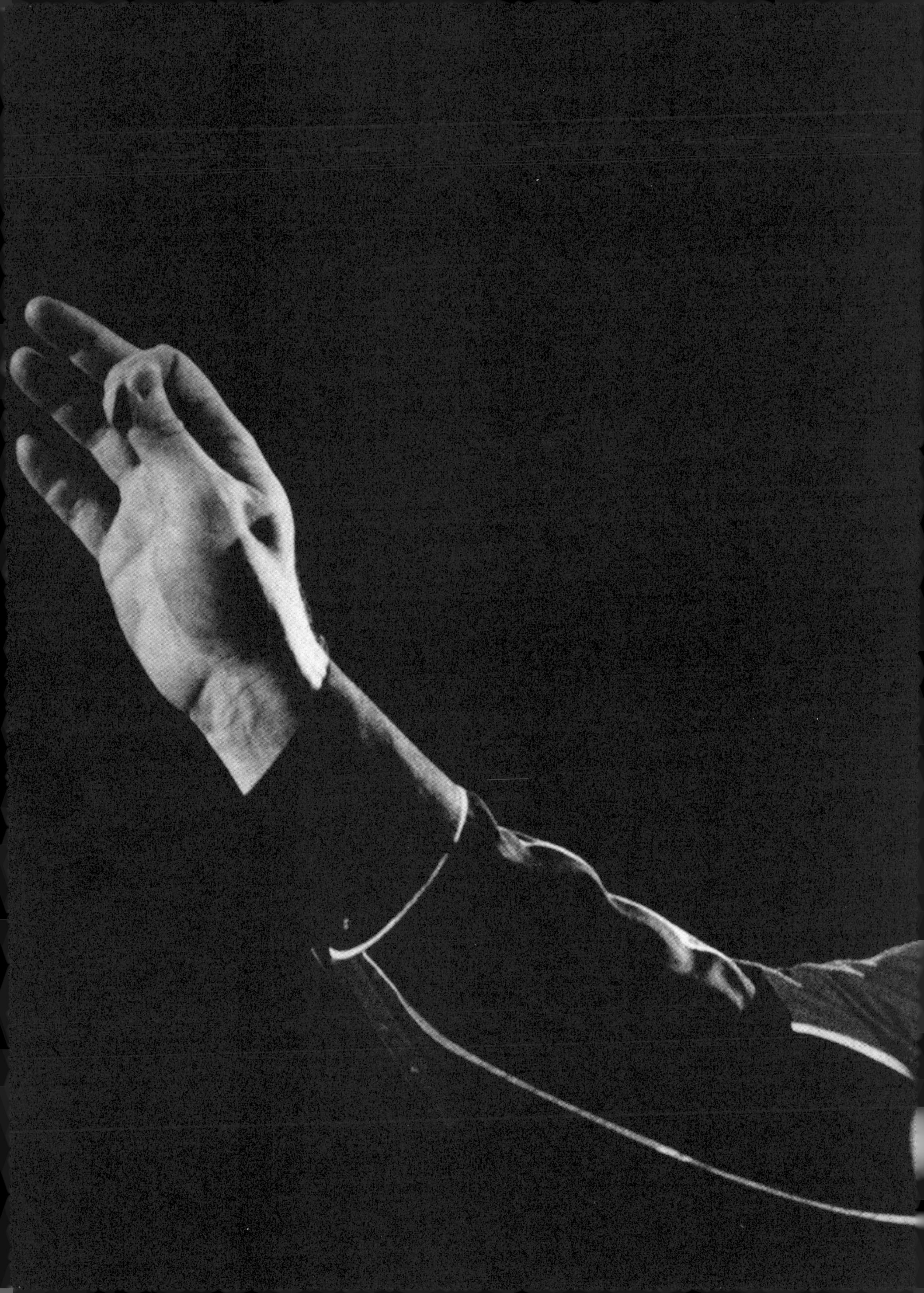

Garth protectively steers Sandy through the backstage crowd.